Praise for *The Sacred Earth*

Assiduously mining the work of an astonishingly varied pantheon of writers — from John Muir to Linda Hogan, John Burroughs to Mary Oliver — and embracing every quality of the natural world from the spiritual to the practical, Jason Gardner has produced an anthology whose words, if we have the wit to listen, will echo in the mind and heart and enlarge our understanding of just where we stand in the great community of life.

— T.H. WATKINS
former editor of *Wilderness* magazine
and Wallace Stegner Professor of Western American Studies
Montana State University

The Sacred Earth is an engaging, uniquely conceived collection of nature writing gems — not long, intricate essays but substantial snippets of poetic prose. As a scholar of nature writing, I enjoyed this fresh approach to many of my favorite writers.

— SCOTT SLOVIC
author of *Seeking Awareness in American Nature Writing*
and director of the Center for Environmental
Arts and Humanities, University of Nevada, Reno

The Sacred Earth

Writers on Nature & Spirit

The Sacred Earth
Writers on Nature & Spirit

Edited by Jason Gardner
Foreword by David Brower

NEW WORLD LIBRARY
NOVATO, CALIFORNIA

New World Library
14 Pamaron Way
Novato, California 94949

Cover design: Alexandra Honig

Cover photo: Copyright © 1988 by Galen Rowell / Mountain Light
　　　　　　　Reflection Pond at dawn, Denali National Park, Alaska

Text design and typography: Jason Gardner

Illustrations: Denise Gardner

Permission acknowledgments on page 165 are an extension of the copyright page.

Library of Congress Cataloging-in-Publication Data

The sacred earth : writers on nature & spirit / edited by Jason Gardner ;
　　foreword by David Brower.
　　　　　p.　　　　　cm.
Includes bibliographical references and index.
ISBN 1-57731-068-3 (alk. paper)
1. Nature. 2. Nature—Psychological aspects. I. Gardner, Jason, 1969–　.
QH81.S194 1998
508—dc21　　　　　　　　　　　　　　　　98-23015
　　　　　　　　　　　　　　　　　　　　　　CIP

First printing, October 1998

ISBN 1-57731-068-3

Printed in Canada on acid-free, recycled paper

Distributed to the trade by Publishers Group West

10　9　8　7　6　5　4　3　2　1

To Denise Gardner and Maureen Phelan
for books and inspiration

CONTENTS

FOR THOSE OF US WHO CARE FOR AN EARTH not encompassed by machines, a world of textures, tastes, and sounds other than those that we have engineered, there can be no questions of simply abandoning literacy, of turning away from all writing. Our task, rather, is that of *taking up* the written word, with all of its potency, and patiently, carefully, writing language back into the land. Our craft is that of releasing the budded, earthly intelligence of our words, freeing them to respond to the speech of the things themselves — to the green uttering-forth of leaves from the spring branches. It is the practice of spinning stories that have the rhythm and lilt of the local soundscape, tales for the tongue, tales that want to be told, again and again, sliding off the digital screen and slipping off the lettered page to inhabit these coastal forests, those whispering grasslands and valleys and swamps. Finding phrases that place us in contact with the trembling neck-muscles of a deer holding its antlers high as it swims toward the mainland, or with the ant dragging a scavenged rice-grain through the grasses. Planting words, like seeds, under rocks and fallen logs — letting language take root, once again, in the earthen silence of shadow and bone and leaf.

— DAVID ABRAM
The Spell of the Sensuous

Foreword

THIS BOOK IS NO SUBSTITUTE FOR BEING OUTSIDE. But it will give a perspective on being outside that isn't always easy to achieve. As someone who edited books for the Sierra Club and the University of California, I am heartened to see so many literary highlights from so many of my favorite authors, laid out to let us readers dabble in their work as we meander in the woods or pause on the trail — to allow us to find the writers who speak to us. Take them slowly; together, they're a rich offering that deserves some pondering. Much more than a fine beginner's sampling of nature writing, *The Sacred Earth* is a penetrating collection of crystalline prose presented as poetry, circling and building and creeping up on us. In the end, it may indeed change our view of the earth and our place on it.

These passages come from many perspectives, some that pat each other on the back in agreement, some that vehemently but respectfully contradict; some rightly serious, some rightly lending humor to our predicament. Its passages range from artful narratives of what it's like to climb a mountain, to revelations about the physical mountain itself, to insightful thoughts on what mountains mean to us, to instructions for learning to think like a mountain, as Aldo Leopold proposed. Call it a well-magnified microcosm of the wild and our varying experiences in it. It shows what the wild can do for our spirit, and even how we can work out a successful relationship with nature.

I once wrote, "To me, God and Nature are synonymous, and neither could wait the billions of years before man arrived to decide what to look like. . . . I have as much trouble comprehending Creation as I do comprehending what it was created out of. I like mystery, the unending search for truth, the truth of beauty. I would have no use for pearly gates and streets of gold if canyon wrens were not admitted."

Religion is sometimes in our way, rather than an aid to us in our search for a truth grounded in the splendor of mountains, the seas, the open land, and life itself. But religion can, and in many traditions does, help us in our search for the truths of nature. And some spiritual sense of nature may be, as this book suggests, necessary for us to halt our thoughtless misuse of the planet. We don't have to agree on what spirituality means. It may simply be a search for personal truth that pays attention to what the world around us has to say. Readers will recognize that search in these passages and in turn will be inspired in their own search.

Enjoy this book for what it is: a trailhead to further exploration in the marvelous realm of nature writing; a totem to aid us in finding and cultivating perspectives that touch our own, sometimes buried, intuitive understandings of what's right; and a reminder to urge us on in repairing the damage we've caused and no longer need to.

— DAVID R. BROWER
Berkeley, July 1998

Acknowledgments

Several comprehensive anthologies of nature writing were absolutely essential in guiding my reading, lending historical scope to the selections, as well as helping to provide essential biographical information: *The Norton Book of Nature Writing*, edited by Robert Finch and John Elder; *This Incomparable Lande: A Book of American Nature Writing*, edited by Thomas J. Lyon; *The Nature Reader*, edited by Daniel Halpern and Dan Frank; *Sisters of the Earth*, edited by Lorraine Anderson; *Words from the Land*, edited by Stephen Trimble; and the Sierra Club's annual *American Nature Writing* anthologies, edited by John A. Murray.

I would like to thank Maureen Phelan for her encouragement and feedback; Joe Durepos for wise advice, mentorship, and friendship; my sister, Danielle Gardner, who's out in the world doing what this book talks about; my father, Philip Gardner, for heartfelt encouragement, generous support, and a sharp editorial eye; and my mother, Denise Gardner, for her reading advice, crafty dingbats, and love for the wild.

Thank you to everyone I work with at New World Library: Becky Benenate, Marc Allen, Munro Magruder, and Victoria Williams-

Clarke have all contributed significantly and graciously to this book. Aaron Kenedi and Alexandra Honig worked passionately on the cover and indulged my eccentric tastes. Thanks also to Tona Pearce Myers, Marjorie Conte, Dean Campbell, Amy Garretson, Michael Rozendal, Cathy Bodenman, Dan Couvillon, and Kristin Wolfe. Everyone's support is much appreciated. Charlie Frago and Thia Boggs offered sheer enthusiasm along the way. Chris Jones gave my introduction a professional edit. It was an honor to work with David Brower and Mikhail Davis at Earth Island Institute. And many thanks to Kurt Redenbo at the Wilderness Society for his flexibility and enthusiasm. The Society deserves everyone's support.

Most of all, thank you to all the authors in this book, many of whom offered the use of their writing at no cost to help the Wilderness Society. Obviously, this book's worth lies in their talent and wisdom.

And along with those thanks, a quick apology to those writers who belong here, but because of some fault of my own, I wasn't able to include — John McPhee, Ann Zwinger, Farley Mowat, and many others come to mind. This isn't a comprehensive collection, but a very personal one.

Introduction

I T'S DIFFICULT TO VIEW THE WORLD outside our human context. Staying alive and paying the bills both require our attention squarely fixed on our own business. Our sprawling cities and suburbs are wonderful and frightening tributes to creative self-absorption. In them, we spend our microscheduled days bustling between work and the endless details of our private lives, turning in our moments of rest to the buzzing distractions of television and computers — all accelerating toward some ultimate, unseen fulfillment of convenience and hyperreality. Little encourages us to pause and look around, much less question the end goal of all our busyness. Anything slower than the quick cuts of TV commercials is overwhelmed by our impatience and short attention. Unfortunately, we might be missing something important — to our happiness *and* to our survival.

The purpose of this book is to help remind us. Excerpted from the work of many of our best contemporary American nature writers — as well as some biologists, activists, and academics — these passages revolve around nature and its connection with the slippery, difficult notion of spirit. Like other overused and commercialized words, spirit has lost some of its meaning, as well as taken on a lot of new meaning. Although it is often associated with the *super*natural — transcendence beyond this world — in this book its meaning is tied more simply to the *natural*. One dictionary defines spirit as, "an animating or vital principle held to give life to physical organisms." Although some writers presented here might squirm at this definition, most might agree to root spirit in life — the teeming soil, the growing trees, the depth of the eyes. They might also extend this notion beyond what we recognize as alive to include *everything*: wind, water, even geological formations. Whether linked to religious beliefs about God, as in Christianity, or to cultivating awareness, as in Buddhism, here, spirit recognizes the world as sacred, and creates our responsibility to treat it with love, to consider it invaluable beyond its relation to people.

The passages in *The Sacred Earth* are short but substantial. Most present whole ideas, even though they are pulled from the larger arguments they serve. These passages may cater to our ever-shortening attention spans, but they also invite us toward a way of viewing the world that is increasingly difficult.

Our relationship with the natural world is maddeningly complicated. When considering the environment and our effect on it, we often seem paralyzed between self-protecting delusion and occasional, maybe realistic despair. In one moment, as we open a newspaper, an international pact to curb global warming brings unexpected hope. In the next, as we turn the page, we are stunned to learn that across the globe 150 acres of rainforest disappear every minute.

The past few decades *have* spawned a powerful environmental movement, with dedicated activists achieving tremendous progress. And where the idea of the environment barely existed thirty years ago, we now cultivate environmental awareness in kindergardeners. Yet for all our progress, it often seems that political environmentalism has failed against enormous odds — co-opted by money-driven politics or corporations seeking green PR, or, like many human activities, splintered into bickering factions. Environmentalism has made enormous inroads, but to the economic/corporate establishment, it often remains a cultural stereotype or a cranky political lobby — a hand-wringing relic of the sixties or an idealistic threat to profit and growth.

Whether we see the future as hopeful or bleak, increasingly, what seems missing from our political approach to the environment — and to nature itself — is a *spiritual* dimension. We need to develop a deep understanding of why it is morally important to consider other species in our profit and loss equations.

Many have recently championed economic solutions to saving the environment. Writers and economists like Paul Hawken and Herman Daly have rightly called for incorporating the real costs of pollution and consumerism into economic models. But political reform falls far short of necessary change. As long as we view the soil, water, plants, and animals through an economic lens, as jobs, or resources for consumption, and not as essential parts of what makes us whole, we will ultimately fail to understand our right and responsibility: to extend our concern for ourselves into a concern for everything, and to dispense with the notion that saving the natural world somehow compromises our interests.

Throughout human history, many understood this spiritual necessity. For most indigenous cultures, the natural world was their first and foremost teacher. Human life and nonhuman life were often indistinguishable. But, probably beginning with the advent of agriculture about 10,000 years ago, and continuing as we pulled away from the earth on the back of technology, we slowly lost our intuitive understanding of that connection. Today, we have all but severed it as consumer capitalism becomes the predominant force guiding human behavior. As many have said, technology has become our new deity; our faith lies in the power of our own intelligence.

But even as we severed this connection, softer voices in Western culture resisted the blind force of industrial economies and pointed to the shadow side of embracing a technological life. From Jean-Jacques Rousseau to Charles Dickens, writers and thinkers confronted civilization's unthinking destruction and the meteoric growth of industrialization. In America, Thoreau and Emerson reacted by criticizing the rise of mechanization and by celebrating the wild. Adding to the words of the European Romantics, their voices both profoundly influenced American thought and paved the way for an American environmentalism infused with spiritual understanding.

Indeed, whatever its political shortcomings, our nation's environmental philosophy rests on the solid foundations of humble preservation and spirituality. These notions are also the foundations of an eloquent new American environmental voice — echoing and building upon the older awareness of Thoreau, Emerson, Whitman, Muir, and Leopold — to combat Western culture's economic myopia. In broad terms, this surge of environmental thought — what writer Mark Dowie calls the "Fourth Wave" of American environmentalism — reaches beyond a human-centered or anthropocentric philosophy to embrace all life. In this sense, while still political, it is both ethical and spiritual.

Many of this movement's underpinnings are expressed directly through the genre of nature writing. The American nature writers in this book often explore outside the realm of political considerations, where we understand through direct contact with the world. Instead of only railing against man's selfish obsessions, they often provide new models for living — new awarenesses that both look back to past attitudes of humility and ahead to new understanding afforded by the science of ecology. While not always directly confronting politics, the ramifications of their perspectives are inherently political. The poet Gary Snyder, for example, seeks to fuse the spirituality of Zen Buddhism, Native American ritual, and deep ecology philosophy into a new ethos that gives Americans the chance to become native to the continent they inhabit — what Snyder calls *Turtle Island*.

Others, like Father Thomas Berry, seek to meld the religious notions of the sacred and profane that have restricted our understanding of nature or allowed us to view it and its creatures solely as resources for our use. Berry's goal is to create a theology that acknowledges the earth as our sculpting influence and source. With him, a growing group of Christians and Jews are rejecting the historical misuse of their religious traditions as a basis for environmental abuse. What Roderick Nash has called the "greening of religion" is under way and is one of this book's main concerns: reconnecting human spirituality with the earth.

Most of the authors in this book — a very personal and incomplete selection — are rooted in the literature of nature writing. Joyce Carol Oates has written that nature "inspires a painfully limited set of responses in 'nature writers' — REVERENCE, AWE, PIETY, MYSTICAL ONENESS." While this criticism fails to recognize the genre's rich variety of voices — or the humor of Ed Abbey and Jim Harrison — Oates correctly identifies an un-self-consciousness that sometimes flies in the face of literary sensibilities that solely value sophistication or detached irony. Nature writing can be intensely personal — heavy with a mysticism that may sound overblown to ears tuned to human concerns. But making the point about what's at stake may justify a more direct, reverential, sometimes somber tone.

Sweeping nature writers to the margins of literature is a mistake. Jim Harrison says that Wyoming writer C.L. Rawlins has argued that the term "nature writing," is like saying "water swimming" — that "we are nature, too...." Indeed, most of the work in this book jumps right out of the "nature writing" pigeonhole to strike deeper than we might first expect. While some of these writings may sound idealistic or anachronistic when compared with modern literary sensibilities, they also encompass more of the world than most of the books written today about human manners and affairs. They often directly examine life's inescapable complexities and darkness. As Gary Snyder writes, "Life in the wild is not just eating berries in the sunlight."

Nor is any optimism mustered in these passages naive. It is often guided by an ethical mandate to continue, against pessimism, to work for good and beauty. As writer Peter Matthiessen, a major voice in this book, once said about social action, "You can make a little betterment here, a little solace there, but it's not very much. Nonetheless you have to do it. *You have to do it.* I passionately think that. We all must make an effort for the betterment of mankind, even though we know it won't do any good." [Emphasis added.]

More often, however, these writings put social and political concerns aside to express wonder at the earth's beauty. As the poet

Mary Oliver celebrates the infinite forms of our world, she asks, "How can we stop looking? How can we turn away?" Conveying the beauty of these forms and reminding us to look with fresh eyes is the task of writers in *Experience* and *Texture* — two of this book's four sections.

Experience is concerned with direct human experience and description. It serves as a portal for increasing our awareness, through the trained observation and storytelling of adventurers, scientists, and writers. Often, as with Peter Matthiessen's passages from *The Snow Leopard*, the prose captures reality with the spare clarity of poetry. Many selections share with the reader the drama and epiphany of direct personal experience. Here we sit with Matthiessen on the side of a Himalayan mountain or lie under an oak tree during a windstorm with Walt Whitman.

Texture is composed of explorations of the physical, the textures of our universe, the spirit present in the world's objects. "The senses long to sense objects and things on their own," Robert Bly writes in his anthology of poetry *News of the Universe*, which chronicles humankind's alienation from nature and its subsequent emerging recognition of nonhuman consciousnesses. These passages in *Texture* are the prose equivalent of what Bly calls "object or thing poetry," created through "the ability to observe, to use the terrific energy of the eyes, to pay attention to something besides one's own subjectivity." Texture may be the best demonstration of cultivating awareness, and expressing that awareness in writing. As Nobel laureate poet Czeslaw Milosz writes in his collection of international poetry *A Book of Luminous Things:* "When the Japanese poet Bashō advised a poet describing a pine to learn from the pine, he wanted to say that contemplation of a thing — a reverent and pious approach to it — is a prerequisite of true art." In *Texture*, Wendell Berry notices the process of decomposition in the bottom of a bucket and Thomas Merton listens to the music of rain in the woods. *Texture* also includes passages about animals — a difficult distinction. (Ravens and porpoises are hardly objects, but they are strands in the fiber of the world.)

Practice explores the ethics and morality of our developing relationship with the earth. Perhaps the most scolding of the sections — and most likely to stir disagreement — these passages can serve as guideposts as we strive for spiritual understanding. More concerned with today's political and social situation but also abstract philosophy, in *Practice* Edward O. Wilson describes the power of the evolutionary perspective and Barry Lopez probes the violence inherent in the circle of life and death.

Belief is the culmination of this book's purpose: to rediscover and reconnect our spirituality with the natural world. Many of these passages speak without the film that human preoccupations can build on our awareness. They view the world through perspectives other than our own. They speak, through devoted effort, about recognizing the extraordinary nature of every aspect of existence. Here we find anthropologist and writer Richard Nelson viewing a forest as a living cathedral, in the manner of the Koyukon people of the Arctic, or Annie Dillard stressing the importance of serving witness to the world's gratuitous beauty.

While this book focuses on contemporary writers — reaching back to Aldo Leopold and Rachel Carson — a few of their 19th century ancestors begin and end each section: Whitman, Emerson, John Burroughs, Thoreau, and Ohiyesa.

Some activists might find it indulgent to sit back and read

about the world's beauty as it is being destroyed — when action seems so important. But as Alaskan poet John Haines writes in his essay "Shadows and Vistas," words are essential to our understanding, as explanations and as reminders:

> You may ask what these remarks of mine have to do with immediate politics and practical tasks — the issues, the problems that many of you understand as well or better than I do. And I have no ready answer, no claim that poetic imagery, the personal mythologies of which a writer is sometimes the master, can solve anything. And yet without that dimension of imagination, the instilled power to think and to visualize that poetry, for example, nourishes in us, the solutions, the resolved difficulties seem bound to lack a necessary human element.
>
> So it is a matter of language also, of words common and uncommon, that with something of their original freshness and power have the ability to restore a much-needed sense of reality and reveal to us a few essential things with clarity and concreteness.

These passages, like Haines's poetry, serve a purpose beyond expressing beauty. While compiling this book, I experienced the familiar feeling of losing sight of my purpose if I spent too long in urban surroundings, filled with the typical preoccupations. We all experience this. Moments of clarity and awareness don't last. We need reminders to knock us back into thinking about and observing life in a way that is antithetical to modern life. When feeling like I would much rather watch TV than pick up a book of nature writing, I came to realize that a short hike in the Oakland Hills near where I live would rekindle my enthusiasm. After an afternoon in the Redwoods, I would return rejuvenated, with a reminder of what we are losing physically, and losing touch with, fresh in my mind. These words serve the same purpose. We need constant reminders — amid the very real concerns of money, family, and work — of that important part of what makes life worth living. We need constant reminders of what will bring us satisfaction — not only *to* bring us satisfaction but to fill us with a motivating rage about our misdirection. While I hoped to choose mostly inspiring, positive selections for this book, they should not distract from the crucial task before us: turning our perspective to the astounding diversity around us and reestablishing our familiarity with and reverence for the spiritual presence of the earth.

— JASON GARDNER

References

Bly, Robert, ed. *News of the Universe: Poems of Twofold Consciousness*. San Francisco: Sierra Club Books, 1980.

Brower, David. *Let the Mountains Talk, Let the Rivers Run: A Call to Those Who Would Save the Earth*. San Francisco: HarperCollinsWest, 1995.

Dowie, Mark. *Losing Ground: American Environmentalism at the Close of the Twentieth Century*. Cambridge, Massachusetts: MIT Press, 1995.

Halpern, Daniel, & Dan Frank, eds. *The Nature Reader*. Hopewell, New Jersey: Ecco Press, 1997.

Milosz, Czeslaw, ed. *A Book of Luminous Things: An International Anthology of Poetry*. New York: Harcourt Brace & Company, 1996.

Murray, John A., ed. *American Nature Writing 1995*. San Francisco: Sierra Club Books, 1995.

Shainberg, Lawrence. "Emptying the Bell: An Interview with Peter Matthiessen," *Tricycle: The Buddhist Review*. Fall 1993.

The Sacred Earth

Writers on Nature & Spirit

Experience

As I came home through the woods with my string of fish, trailing my pole, it being now quite dark, I caught a glimpse of a woodchuck stealing across my path, and felt a strange thrill of savage delight, and was strongly tempted to seize and devour him raw; not that I was hungry then, except for that wildness which he represented. Once or twice, however, while I lived at the pond, I found myself ranging in the woods, like a half-starved hound, with a strange abandonment, seeking some kind of venison which I might devour, and no morsel could have been too savage for me. The wildest scenes had become unaccountably familiar. I found in myself, and still find, an instinct toward a higher, or, as it is named, spiritual life, as do most men, and another toward a primitive rank and savage one, and I reverence them both. I love the wild not less than the good.

— HENRY DAVID THOREAU
Walden

I AM UP BEFORE THE SUN, AND MAKE A FIRE. The water boils as the sun ignites the peaks, and we breakfast in sunshine on hot tea and porridge. A nutcracker is rasping in the pines, and soon the crows come, down the morning valley; cawing, they hide among long shimmering needles, then glide in, bold, to walk about in the warming scent of resin, dry feet scratching on the bark of fallen trees.

Since Jang-bu cannot reach Tarakot before the evening, we have time. I walk barefoot in the grass, spreading my gear with ceremony: today, for the first time in weeks, everything will dry, a great event in expedition life. Then with my stave I prop my pack upright and sit back against the mountainside, my face in cold shade and hot sun on my arms and belly.

Pine needles dance in a light breeze against the three white sister peaks to the northwest. I sit in silence, lost in the burning hum of mountain bees. An emerald butterfly comes to my knee to dry its wings, gold wings with black specks above, white polka dots beneath. Through the frozen atmospheres, the sun is burning.

In the clearness of this Himalayan air, mountains draw near, and in such splendor, tears come quietly to my eyes and cool on my sun-burned cheeks. This is not mere soft-mindedness, nor am I all that silly with the altitude. My head has cleared in these weeks free of intrusions — mail, telephones, people and their needs — and I respond to things spontaneously, without defensive or self-conscious screens. Still, all this *feeling* is astonishing: not so long ago I could say truthfully that I had not shed a tear in twenty years.

— PETER MATTHIESSEN
The Snow Leopard

IN THE AUTUMN OF 1985, a strong hurricane ripped across suburban Long Island, where I was then living as a student. For several days afterward much of the populace was without electricity; power lines were down, telephone lines broken, and the roads were strewn with toppled trees. People had to walk to their jobs, and to whatever shops were still open. We began encountering each other on the streets, "in person" instead of by telephone. In the absence of automobiles and their loud engines, the rhythms of crickets and birdsong became clearly audible. Flocks were migrating south for the winter, and many of us found ourselves simply listening, with new and childlike curiosity, to the ripples of song in the still-standing trees and the fields. And at night the sky was studded with stars! Many children, their eyes no longer blocked by the glare of houselights and streetlamps, saw the Milky Way for the first time, and were astonished. For those few days and nights our town became a community aware of its place in an encompassing cosmos. Even our noses seemed to come awake, the fresh smells from the ocean somehow more vibrant and salty. The breakdown of our technologies had forced a return to our senses, and hence to the natural landscape in which those senses are so profoundly embedded. We suddenly found ourselves inhabiting a sensuous world that had been waiting, for years, at the very fringe of our awareness, an intimate terrain infused with birdsong, salt spray, and the light of stars.

— DAVID ABRAM
The Spell of the Sensuous

I DELIGHT IN THE SPARE LANDSCAPE out the plane window — ice oceans and ice mountains and clouds full of ice. So much of what Americans live with is an economic landscape — malls, stores, and movie theaters, ski slopes and theme parks — in which one's relationship to place has to do with boredom, undisciplined need, and envy. The Arctic's natural austerity is richness enough, its physical clarity a form of voluptuousness. Who needs anything more?

The first time I visited Greenland was two summers after a near fatal lightning strike. My heart had stopped and started several times, and the recovery from ten thousand volts of electricity surging through my brain took years. To live nose to nose with death pruned away emotional edacity and the presumption of a future, even another sunrise. Life was an alternating current of dark and light. I lost consciousness hundreds of times, and death's presence was always lurking — a black form in the corner. Life was the light hovering at the top of the sea.

Greenland's treeless, icebound landscape appealed to me so much then that now, three years later, I've come back. Its continuously shifting planes of light are like knives thrown in a drawer. They are the layered instruments that carve life out of death into art and back to life. They teach me how to see.

— GRETEL EHRLICH
"Cold Comfort: Looking for the Sun in Greenland's Endless Night"
from *Harper's*

I WAS SITTING OUT BACK ON MY 33,000-ACRE TERRACE, shoeless and shirtless, scratching my toes in the sand and sipping on a tall iced drink, watching the flow of evening over the desert. Prime time: the sun very low in the west, the birds coming back to life, the shadows rolling for miles over rock and sand to the very base of the brilliant mountains. I had a small fire going near the table — not for heat or light but for the fragrance of the juniper and the ritual appeal of the clear flames. For symbolic reasons. For ceremony. When I heard a faint sound over my shoulder I looked and saw a file of deer watching from fifty yards away, three does and a velvet-horned buck, all dark against the sundown sky. They began to move. I whistled and they stopped again, staring at me. "Come on over," I said, "have a drink." They declined, moving off with casual, unhurried grace, quiet as phantoms, and disappeared beyond the rise. Smiling, thoroughly at peace, I turned back to my drink, the little fire, the subtle transformations of the immense landscape before me. On the program: rise of the full moon.

— EDWARD ABBEY
Desert Solitaire

ONE JULY WEEKEND MY PARTNER AND I tried the Chouinard-Herbert route on Sentinel Rock, a 1,700-foot face normally done in two days. Mid-morning on the second day, after a bivouac on a ledge, we killed our last bottle of water — we had badly miscalculated our need — and climbed ahead into the ninety-degree afternoon. We became so weak we couldn't finish the climb by dark, though we had reached the easy ledges near the top. We spent another night, sleeping like stones as the brightest colors I have ever seen flamed through my dreams. In the morning we made our way to the top, there to find an enormous orange-barked ponderosa pine, standing alone. It seemed to glow from within, a tree but more than a tree, an emblem of being itself. And the stream we finally came to, after what seemed hours of stumbling descent down the dry gully behind Sentinel, was no ordinary stream with a fringe of plants — how *green* those plants were — but the very Garden. We knelt there, feeling the icy glow of water inside us with our booming and skittering hearts.

— JOHN DANIEL
The Trail Home

ONCE I CLIMBED BRANDON MOUNTAIN WITH A FRIEND. It was a fine bright day as we set out from the bridge at Brandon Creek. By the time we had ascended a thousand feet, clouds had rolled in from the sea. At 2,000 feet we entered an unbroken cover of cloud. At the saddle between Brandon and Masatiompan we cautiously hesitated, turned south, and moved carefully along the ridge toward the summit, mindful of the steep cliffs that fell away sharply to the east. And then an amazing thing happened! As we approached the summit of the mountain, our heads popped out of the clouds; for a moment our decapitated heads rested on white cotton like laboratory specimens. Another step — shoulders emerged. Then torsos. Step by step we lifted our bodies out of white fleece into a sky of stunning clarity and perfect blue. The summit of Brandon Mountain was an island of rock that protruded ten feet above the cloud, a hundred square feet of solidity in a universe of air. From horizon to horizon the top of the cloud stretched as smooth and uninterrupted as the surface of the sea. White cottony cloud! It seemed as if we could have stepped off our island onto it. It seemed as if we could have walked across it to those other islands to the south, the distant summits of McGillicudy's Reeks. A temperature inversion of remarkable definition had reduced our world to a clean slate, a featureless interface of blue and white, a *tabula rasa*, a fresh creation. A borrowed metaphor came to mind: *Knowledge is an island surrounded by a sea of mystery*. On Brandon's cloud-truncated summit, that metaphor was made startlingly real.

— CHET RAYMO
Honey from Stone

MY WIFE, JOANNE, BOTH ENHANCES AND DISTRACTS from what I see in nature alone. She asks questions and enthuses; we talk. In striving to articulate what we feel, how each of us reacts to the land, we use language earlier than I would alone to recreate the feel of light on sandstone or the smell of cliffrose. In some ways, I use up the words by sharing the experience; alone, I hoard them, secreting them away in my journal. Talking with the woman I love about the places we pass through makes the experiences warmer, simpler. The landscape becomes a part of everyday life, and I have trouble separating from it sufficiently to describe it as a writer.

At the same time Joanne sees what I do not. She points out details I would miss. She questions things I take for granted; interested though untrained in natural history, she asks about birds and behavior and ecological patterns in an observant way that demands clarity and understanding in order to answer. She makes me think beyond where I might have stopped.

On the Black Rock Desert, we once took turns leaving each other. One of us would step out of the vehicle with no gear — no pack, no camera, no water bottle — and simply stand there in T-shirt, shorts, and thongs, with the silence ringing our ears, while the other drove out of sight. Each of us had a few minutes alone, turning in circles, trying to orient ourselves in the endless miles of barren clay — a near-impossible task. The disorientation was stunning; it was delightful.

When Joanne drove back, the distinction between aloneness and sharing overwhelmed me. The difference was palpable, although both can bring joy.

— STEPHEN TRIMBLE
The Geography of Childhood

THE NIGHTS AT SHEY ARE RIGID, UNDER RIGID STARS; the fall of a wolf pad on the frozen path might be heard up and down the canyon. But a hard wind comes before the dawn to rattle the tent canvas, and this morning it is clear again, and colder. At daybreak, the White River, just below, is sheathed in ice, with scarcely a murmur from the stream beneath.

The two ravens come to tritons on the gompa roof. *Gorawk, gorawk*, they croak, and this is the name given to them by the sherpas. Amidst the prayer flags and great horns of Tibetan argali, the gorawks greet first light with an odd musical double note — *a-ho* — that emerges as if by miracle from those ragged throats. Before sunrise every day, the great black birds are gone, like the last tatters of departing night.

— PETER MATTHIESSEN
The Snow Leopard

WE HEARD A COYOTE YIPPING in the meadow yesterday afternoon, barking in the wind. The tops of all the trees were swaying gently, but when I looked at the wall of the forest, it seemed that the trees were all standing at attention, standing there watching me, and barely moving — just up high. Cottonwood puffballs blew through the field. The woods will either have me or they'll send me home. Every small sight, every small action, counts. That coyote's barks are accumulating, becoming part of my life, and I am turning away from my old life and walking into a new one....

— RICK BASS
Winter

AT THE HIGH POINT OF THE BLUFF, where the road began a slow curve and descent, I stopped to look out over the river in the growing dusk. Light lay over the water, on the islands and the hills of the distance, so pervasive and steeped in its yellowness, it was hard to tell if that light came from the evening sky or welled up from somewhere in the autumn earth itself.

I listened to the pebbly sound of the river falling through diminished channels below me. And for a long moment I felt myself a part of that landscape with its shaggy, black islands and pale sandbars, one with the coppery gleam of water coiling and darkening, the distant country of night.

— JOHN HAINES
The Stars, the Snow, the Fire

THOUSANDS OF SMALL FISH are moving along in the shallows: a flock, a flight under the weight of the water, dipping and rising, loose-spined; their fins, rowing, are minute and precise; they are energy-packets; six would fit into a thimble, all gauze and glaze, and all translucent — the pipeline of appetite clear in each body. Thousands and thousands — a throng of rainbows, a pod, an enormous pack, yet they swing along as a single rainbow, one wing, one thing, one traveler. Their mouths are open, fierce colanders scooping in the diatoms. They turn to the right, the left. They dash and hover. . . .

It is summer, the long twilight. I stare and stare into the water. I say to myself, *which one am I?*

— MARY OLIVER
Blue Pastures

ONE SPRING EVENING A COUPLE YEARS AGO, I was sitting in the brown leather chair in the living room reading the newspaper and minding my own business when I became aware that I was no longer alone.

Looking up, I discovered that the three big windows that run from floor to ceiling were covered with frogs.

There were hundreds of them, inch-long frogs with delicate webbed feet whose fingerlike toes ended in round pads that enabled them to cling to the smooth surface of the glass. From their toe structure, size and light-colored bellies, I supposed them to be spring peepers, *Hyla crucifer*, and went outside for a closer look. I had to be careful where I put my feet, for the grass in front of the windows was thick with frogs, waiting in patient ranks to move up to the lighted surface of the glass. Sure enough, each pinkish-brownish frog had a back criss-crossed with the dark markings that give the species its scientific name. I had not known before that they were attracted to light.

I let my newspaper go and spent the evening watching them. They did not move much beyond the top of the windows, but clung to the glass or the moldings, seemingly unable to decide what to do next. The following morning they were gone, and I have never seen them at the windows since. It struck me as curious behavior.

— SUE HUBBELL
A Country Year

ON MY TRAVELS IN TIBET I was always delighted by the tradition of sky-burial. The human body is cut up and the bones broken to the marrow and left for animals, mostly birds. Later the bones are pounded and mixed with tsampa — a roasted barley — and again offered to the animals. Finally everything is gone, gone back into the cycle. Recently, when a friend lost her beloved dog, she carried it out to a beautiful view of the mountains, covered it with wild flowers, and left it for the coyotes and ravens and bugs. We should have the courage to do the same for ourselves, to re-enter the great cycle of feeding.

The moose incorporates the willow, taking the life of the willow into its own life, making the wilderness of the willow reincarnate. I kill the moose, its body feeds the willow and grouse wortleberries where it dies, it feeds my body, and in feeding my body, the willow and the moose feed the one billion bacteria that inhabit three inches of my colon, the one million spirochetes that live in my mouth, and the microscopic brontosaurus-like mites that live by devouring the goo on my eyelashes. The great feeding body is the world. It evolved together, mutually, all interdependent, all interrelating ceaselessly, the dust of old stars hurtling through time, and we are the form it chose to make it conscious of itself.

— JACK TURNER
The Abstract Wild

I REMEMBER CAMPING OUT ON A SMALL ISLAND in the lake. We ate freshly caught bass by the campfire. When darkness fell, a shooting star streaked across the sky. I was told of an ancient belief that it was the soul of someone who had just died. We slept under blankets on the ground. Waking up at first light, I saw a fiery red squirrel scolding me from the top of a pine tree, like a little masthead of the dawn.

The trees marched up the hills and moved into abandoned pastures, claiming ancient rights of possession. The white pines, with their long, glistening needles, would swing in limber rhythms with the wind. The heavy boughs of the hemlocks dipped their dark shadows toward the ground and lifted up again. Bordering the lake, where thrushes sang in the evening, the leaves of white birch, gray beech, and maple stirred and danced in the breeze. Varying airs pushed small ripples across the lake causing its surfaces to flash in the sunlight. In sandy shallows close to shore, the sunfish circled, waved their fins, and laid their eggs. Farther out in the waters of that sun- and star-crossed lake were the black or big-mouth bass, like ambient shadows.

— JOHN HAY
A Beginner's Faith in Things Unseen
(Writing about his family's New Hampshire summer home)

THE COMPLEAT TOURIST TOWN. In the restaurants blue gas fires burning under stacks of ceramic logs that look almost real until you get close. Omnipresent in the background that bland tapioca-like sound my wife calls "department-store music." Decor by Holiday Inn — all the motel lobby furnishings, all the restaurant tables and chairs and lighting fixtures, look as though they came from the same factory somewhere in Southern California. Everything designed by a neurotic suffering from a severe case of social irrelevance.

What's the alternative to this comfortable mediocrity? A grand European-style luxury that most of us would not be able to afford? Or a return to the mode of a century ago, coming into a mountain village on horseback, having a cold supper by lamplight in the cabin-kitchen of some morose mountaineer, while savage coon dogs howl, slaver and snarl on the other side of the door, and going to sleep in the early dark on a cornshuck mattress, prey to a host of bloodsucking vermin?

Which would you prefer? Which would I really prefer?

You won't believe me but I'll tell you: I fancy the latter, i.e., the horse, cabin, dogs and bugs.

— EDWARD ABBEY
Appalachian Wilderness: The Great Smokey Mountains

THEN ONE AUGUST NIGHT IN THE DRY SEASON, with the moon down and starlight etching the tops of the trees, everything changed with wrenching suddenness. A great storm came up from the west and moved quickly toward where I sat. It began as a flickering of light on the horizon and a faint roll of thunder. In the course of an hour the lightning grew like a menacing organism into flashes that spread across the sky and illuminated the thunderhead section by section. The sound expanded into focused claps to my left, front, and right. Now the rain came walking through the forest with a hiss made oddly soothing by its evenness of pitch. At this moment the clouds rose straight up and even seemed to tilt a little toward me, like a gigantic cliff about to topple over. The brilliance of the flashes was intimidating. Here, I knew, was the greatest havoc that inanimate nature can inflict in a short span of time: 10,000 volts dropping down an ionizing path at 500 miles an hour and a countersurge in excess of 30,000 amperes back up the path at ten times that speed, then additional back-and-forth surges faster than the eye can follow, all perceived as a single flash and crack of sound. . . .

Large splashing drops turned into sheets of water driven by gusts of wind. I retreated into the camp and waited with my *mateiros* friends under the dripping canvas roof. In a short time leptodactylid frogs began to honk their territorial calls in the forest nearby. To me they seemed to be saying rejoice! rejoice! The powers of nature are within our compass.

For that is the way it is in the nonhuman world. The greatest powers of the physical environment slam into the resilient forces of life and nothing much happens.

— EDWARD O. WILSON
"Storm Over the Amazon," from *Antaeus*

IN NEW ENGLAND ONE WALKS quite gradually into a wood, but not so in the jungle. One steps through the wall of the tropic forest, as Alice stepped through the looking glass; a few steps, and the wall closes behind. The first impression is of the dark, soft atmosphere, an atmosphere which might be described as "hanging," for in the great tangle of leaves and fronds and boles it is difficult to perceive any one plant as a unit; there are only these hanging shapes draped by lianas in the heavy air, as if they had lost contact with the earth. And this feeling is increased by the character of the earth itself, which is quite unlike the thrifty woodland floor at home; here the tree boles erupt out of heaped-up masses of decay, as if the ground might be almost any distance beneath. The trees themselves are so tumultuous and strange that one sees them as a totality, a cumulative effect, scarcely noticing details; there is a strange, evilly spined palm trunk, though, and a crouching plant with gigantic fronds, and a fantastic parasite, like a bundle of long red pipe-cleaners studded with olive nuts, fastened here and there to the high branches, and the looming trunk of a silk-cotton, seen only when one is right on top of it; it soars off through the leathery green canopy overhead....

There came a sudden avalanche of tropical rain, crashing to earth, and immediately, in a small stream, small fish like sunfish leaped and whirled. A water snake, emerald-speckled on a throat distended by what must have been a still-live frog, swam clumsily away, disappearing into a black tunnel where the stream slipped into the jungle wall; at this moment, for the first time, the jungle came into focus for me. I could feel it, hear it, smell it all at once, could believe I was almost there.

— PETER MATTHIESSEN
The Cloud Forest

IT IS RAINING TODAY. The damp creeps in through the cracks in the walls, and the must of soggy timbers mingles with the dank of soggy air. My bones rebel. They, too, are filling with moisture, unseen capillaries drinking their fill and turning white brittleness to a boggy grey.

The cat brushes against me. His insistent warmth conjures images of fireplaces and cozy nooks. But today there is no place to hide. The rain has come calling, and it closes down around us like a curtain made of stone.

It is faceless and indifferent, this rain — devoid of the drama of a mountain squall or the power of a prairie thunderhead. It is nourishing the earth's deeper need. We humans can only survive and endure. . . .

It is good to know such rain. It calls us to examine the landscape of our hearts. Distances are muted and the sounds plunge down from heaven. We are enclosed, at once denied the joy of distant vistas and protected from the intrusions of unseen events. It is now that we truly know ourselves as creatures of the earth: the heavens in their relentless indifference are pounding down upon us with a purpose that transcends our time and scale.

— KENT NERBURN
A Haunting Reverence

A FRIEND OF MINE, A GANGLING MAN who assembles color televisions for a living and who has lost two wives because of his passion for birding, told me about meeting a great horned owl in a tulip tree. He had climbed the tree before dawn to wait to photograph the sunrise over Lake Monroe. There he perched . . . his legs straddling a limb and his back against the trunk. Presently, the branch just above his head shook, as if someone had given it a single karate chop. Looking up, he saw the solemn bird. He was scanning the territory, head tilted forward and slowly pivoting, ear-tufts raised like twin antennae, saucer eyes making a murderous survey of the lakeside. When it spied my friend, the owl glanced casually away, and then did a comical double-take. For a moment the two perchers stared eye-to-eye, the man calculating whether there was light enough for a photo, the bird probably calculating whether this gawky beast would do for breakfast. Evidently deciding no, the owl gave a noncommittal hoot and flew away. My friend was lucky this was a hunting rather than a nesting tree, for had he approached the nest, the bird would probably have mauled him.

— SCOTT RUSSELL SANDERS
"Listening for Owls," from *The Paradise of Bombs*

NATURE LAUGHS AT ME. She's an animal with shining teeth, a mother who doesn't love me. Smoothing her dark skirts, her wild hair blowing free, she asks if I recognize her. No, I murmur, I'm a city boy. When my wife was learning to love the outdoors — as a Girl Scout, in the 4-H club, on camping trips with her family — I was learning to love winding boulevards and tall buildings. On darkened streets, in dingy neighborhoods, I can read the writing on the wall, but I can't make out nature's wild scrawl. I confuse rustling leaves with the looming presence of a madman; the smell of black dirt with the hot, moist breath of a bear.

Large drops of rain hit the tent as the wind picks up. Staring wide-eyed into the darkness, I remember the words of anthropologist Richard Nelson. Nature isn't merely created by God, Nelson writes, nature *is* God. When we walk in the woods we can experience the sacredness with our entire body, breathe it, drink the sacred water as a living communion, touch the living branch. Yet here, in the darkness, on this billion-year-old mountain, it's not God I crave but the safety of home, the way a drowning swimmer craves land. I feel as if I've been stranded in an immense alien mind I'll never understand, lost in a billion-year-old story in which human history is a footnote.

— SY SAFRANSKY
"Trail's End," from *Four in the Morning*

LATER THERE WERE NIGHT WALKS in Paris and London, Costa Rica and Ecuador, where I flushed a tree full of vultures on a cliff far above the Pacific swells; Moscow and Leningrad, where I walked the Neva embankment, thinking about my distant cousin, the poet Sergei Yesenin; the beach north of Mombasa, where tiny, finger-sized poisonous snakes tried to get in my pant cuffs; Rio, where you can store minuscule bikinis in your cheeks like a Buddha squirrel. Foreign oceans have the aura of countries that cartographers have forgotten to put on maps.

At present I have tried to stop everything, pure and simple, stuffing time and memory into a custom-blown fishbowl from Belgium, but without success. At my cabin, miles from the nearest neighbor in the Upper Peninsula of Michigan, I walk at night when the moon isn't shrouded by the fog or the cold rain that dominates the area — weather that seems to suit my temperament. I hear coyotes, whippoorwills and loons, bears wallowing off through the swamps, and once I heard and saw a timber wolf. If you are bored, strained, lacerated, enervated by the way we live now, I suggest a night walk as far as you can get from a trace of civilization. This form of walking is a dance, and the ghost that follows you, your moon-cast shadow, is your true androgynous parent, bearing within its distinct outline the child who has always directed your every move.

— JIM HARRISON
"Night Walking," from *Just Before Dark*

I AM UP ON MY ELBOWS, and the sliver of the new sun is perched upon my toes. That red shimmering light is ninety-three million miles away, eight light-minutes away. Almost instantly, the sliver becomes reattached to the body of the sun. Now the full solar disk mushrooms from the ridge, fattening until it balances on the skyline like a rolling wheel. The rising takes two minutes — two minutes for the Earth to turn on its axis one-half of a degree. I am flying toward the sun on my bed of stone at a thousand miles per hour. Two minutes from the first instant of dawn and it is fully day. All over Ireland salmon stir in their deep pools. The fair sea pinks shake in their sea-cliff hollows. And suddenly there is a huge booming noise, like a crack of thunder, and my first thought is that I have actually *heard* the sunrise, heard the wrenching report of the sun as it let go of the horizon. I quickly realize that what I have just heard had nothing to do with the sun. It was a sonic boom — a military jet, perhaps, on an early-morning flight to America. But somewhere in the mountains near the foot of Dingle Bay a hawk lets go of its perch and falls onto rising air, even as I fall toward the place on the horizon that has disgorged the sun.

— CHET RAYMO
Honey from Stone

I FINISHED MY WALK ON THE FOREST'S EDGE, where the great music of crashing waves flooded into the tide pools, where wind ruffled devil's club leaves, and hermit thrushes sang. I reminded myself that the wisest, most inspired people I knew had all taken this second path, heading for what I call the Far Outside. It is the path found when one falls into "the naturalist's trance," the hunter's pursuit of wild game, the *curandera*'s search for hidden roots, the fisherman's casting of the net into the current, the water witcher's trust of the forked willow branch, the rock climber's fixation on the slightest details of a cliff face. Why is it that when we are hanging from the cliff — beyond the reach of civilization's safety net, rather than in it — we are most likely to gain the deepest sense of what it is to be alive? Arctic writer-ethnographer Hugh Brody has brooded over this question while working in the most remote human communities and wildest places he can find. There, he admits, "at the periphery is where I can come to understand the central issues of living."

— GARY PAUL NABHAN
Cultures of Habitat

I REMEMBER ONE NIGHT, lying on the moist spring earth beside my mother. The fire of stars stretched away from us, and the mysterious darkness traveled without limit beyond where we lay on the turning earth. I could smell the damp new grass that night, but I could not touch or hold such black immensity that lived above our world, could not contain within myself even a small corner of the universe.

There seemed to be two kinds of people; earth people and those others, the sky people, who stumbled over pebbles while they walked around with their heads in clouds. Sky people loved different worlds than I loved; they looked at nests in treetops and followed the long white snake of vapor trails. But I was an earth person, and while I loved to gaze up at night and stars, I investigated the treasures at my feet, the veined wing of a dragonfly opening a delicate blue window to secrets of earth, a lusterless beetle that drank water thirstily from the tip of my finger and was transformed into sudden green and metallic brilliance. It was enough mystery for me to ponder the bones inside our human flesh, bones that through some incredible blueprint of life grow from a moment's passion between a woman and a man, walk upright a short while, then walk themselves back to dust.

Years later, lost in the woods one New Year's eve, a friend found the way home by following the north star, and I began to think that learning the sky might be a practical thing. But it was the image of the earth from out in space that gave me upward-gazing eyes. It was that same image that gave the sky people an anchor in the world, for it returned us to our planet in a new and loving way.

— LINDA HOGAN
Dwellings

THE QUETZAL IS A SHINING FACET of the great civilization of nature, where the spirit of human life was once inextricable from birds and flowers and tall trees rising from buttressed trunks with branches smothered in bromeliads and epiphytes, a context of growth and sacrifice reaching through intricate shadows toward the sun. In an open clearing at the edge of the forest where the quetzal and his less extravagantly adorned mate were nesting, a wattled bell bird called with a loud, single "bong," which sounded less like a bell than a metal pipe being hit by a hammer. Inside the forest, nightingale thrushes hauntingly sang, like fine instruments being tuned to some ineffable scale; and the last I saw of the quetzal was a shimmering waterfall of color plunging down off a branch to disappear in the darkness made by endless leaves.

To think of the dark and tenacious rainforests in terms of the diversity we say is necessary to natural systems is useful to the conservationist, but it is not enough. We who spend our lives guided only by terms and categories, endless facts and numbers, have not yet recognized the depths that would, if they could, help us out of our simplicity, the lack of diversity in ourselves. The great tropical message is inclusion. The forests, with their endlessly varied functions and differences in form, are statements as to the total involvement of life. They are the original grounds of life's inventions, a great drawing in of all kinds of possibilities, over endless time. Without them, we lose not only their incomparable species but the foundation of shared existence.

— JOHN HAY
The Immortal Wilderness

...PAUL REMARKS THAT HE LIKES THE LOOK of the young trees coming up between the stumps. They are a bushy, bright green — puppies of the plant world. He argues they have a beauty of their own, an intimate charm as worthy of consideration as an old forest. Perhaps ten years old, the young conifers planted on a clearcut have grown up and together in a thick, interwoven carpet that rolls away into the mist.

Of the beauty of young trees healing the human scar, there is no question. On a golden autumn morning, its frost melting and then steaming in the sun, a cut-over and replanted patch west of town shimmers with tinseled light. It is the end of the summer season when Northwest spiders reach their biggest, and here they have woven hundreds of webs, glossy with dew, between the young conifers. The rising sun lights them as if they were made of silver neon. The effect is magical, as if life is physically stitching together the interstices of the vanished big forest, endlessly repairing itself in a cyclical rite of rejuvenation that those who live here argue is as sacred as an ancient grove.

— WILLIAM DIETRICH
The Final Forest

ONE BEAUTIFUL AFTERNOON, cool and moist, with the kind of yellow light that falls on earth in these arid regions, I waited for barn swallows to return from their daily work of food gathering. Inside the tunnel where they live, hundreds of swallows had mixed their saliva with mud and clay, much like the solitary bees, and formed nests that were perfect as a potter's bowl. At five in the evening, they returned all at once, a dark, flying shadow. Despite their enormous numbers and the crowding together of nests, they didn't pause for even a moment before entering the nests, nor did they crowd one another. Instantly they vanished into the nests. The tunnel went silent.

But I knew they were there, filled with the fire of living. And what a marriage of elements was in those nests. Not only mud's earth and water, the fire of sun and dry air, but even the elements contained one another. The bodies of prophets and crazy men were broken down in that soil.

— LINDA HOGAN
Dwellings

I PREFER PLACES VALUED BY NO ONE ELSE. The Upper Peninsula has many of these places that lack the drama and differentiation favored by the garden variety nature buff. I have a personal stump back in a forest clearing. Someone, probably a deerhunter, has left a beer bottle beside the stump. I leave the beer bottle there to conceal the value of the stump.

It took me twenty years to see a timber wolf in the wild. I could have foreshortened this time period by going to Isle Royale or Canada but I wanted to see the wolf as part of a day rather than as a novelty. We startled each other. From this single incident I dreamt I found the wolf with her back broken on a logging road. I knelt down and she went inside me, becoming part of my body and skeleton.

— JIM HARRISON
"Passacaglia on Getting Lost," from *Just Before Dark*

THE SUN IS SHINING AND THE RAIN IS FALLING. We've all seen this happen, but what I mean is both: it is a bright, perfect day, and a fine but heavy rain is falling from a single cloud that's floating meekly across the valley, in no way impeding the bright sunlight all around. A warm spell. The dogs' water did not even freeze in the red metal bowl. I think I am beginning to see a pattern, discern through this rain and sun — that there is no pattern.

— RICK BASS
Winter

THERE IS SO MUCH THAT ENCHANTS ME in this spare, silent place that I move softly so as not to break a spell. Because the taking of life has been forbidden by the Lama of Shey, bharal and wolves alike draw near the monastery. On the hills and in the stone beds of the river are fossils from blue ancient days when all this soaring rock lay beneath the sea. And all about are the prayer stones, prayer flags, prayer wheels, and prayer mills in the torrent, calling on all the elements in nature to join in celebration of the One. What I hear from my tent is a delicate wind-bell and the river from the east, in this easterly wind that may bring a change in the weather. At daybreak, two great ravens come, their long toes scratching on the prayer walls.

— PETER MATTHIESSEN
The Snow Leopard

A DROWSY, HALF-WAKEFUL MENACE WAITS FOR US in the quietness of this world. I have felt it near me while kneeling in the snow, minding a trap on a ridge many miles from home. There, in the cold that gripped my face, in the low, blue light failing around me, and the short day ending, in those familiar and friendly shadows, I was suddenly aware of something that did not care if I lived. Or, as it may be, running the river ice in midwinter: under the sled runners a sudden cracking and buckling that scared the dogs and sent my heart racing. How swiftly the solid bottom of one's life can go.

— JOHN HAINES
The Snow, the Stars, the Fire

WE WERE EATING LUNCH ON A HIGH RIMROCK, at the foot of which a turbulent river elbowed its way. We saw what we thought was a doe fording the torrent, her breast awash in white water. When she climbed the bank toward us and shook out her tail, we realized our error: it was a wolf. A half-dozen others, evidently grown pups, sprang from the willows and all joined in a welcoming mêlée of wagging tails and playful maulings. What was literally a pile of wolves writhed and tumbled in the center of an open flat at the foot of our rimrock.

In those days we had never heard of passing up a chance to kill a wolf. In a second we were pumping lead into the pack, but with more excitement than accuracy: how to aim a steep downhill shot is always confusing. When our rifles were empty, the old wolf was down, and a pup was dragging a leg into impassable slide-rocks.

We reached the old wolf in time to watch a fierce green fire dying in her eyes. I realized then, and have known ever since, that there was something new to me in those eyes — something known only to her and to the mountain. I was young then, and full of trigger-itch; I thought that because fewer wolves meant more deer, that no wolves would mean hunters' paradise. But after seeing the green fire die, I sensed that neither the wolf nor the mountain agreed with such a view.

— ALDO LEOPOLD
A Sand County Almanac

This is the fourth day of a dark northeast storm, wind and rain. Day before yesterday was my birthday. I have now entered on my 60th year. Every day of the storm, protected by overshoes and a waterproof blanket, I regularly come down to the pond, and ensconce myself under the lee of the great oak; I am here now writing these lines. The dark smoke-colored clouds roll in furious silence athwart the sky; the soft green leaves dangle all round me; the wind steadily keeps up its hoarse, soothing music over my head — Nature's mighty whisper. Seated here in solitude I have been musing over my life — connecting events, dates, as links of a chain, neither sadly nor cheerily, but somehow, today here under the oak, in the rain, in an unusually matter-of-fact spirit. But my great oak — sturdy, vital, green — five feet thick at the butt; I sit a great deal near or under him. Then the tulip tree near by — the Apollo of the woods — tall and graceful, yet robust and sinewy, inimitable in hang of foliage and throwing-out of limb; as if the beauteous, vital, leafy creature could walk, if it only would. (I had a sort of dream-trance the other day, in which I saw my favorite trees step out and promenade up, down and around, very curiously — with a whisper from one, leaning down as he passed me, "We do all this on the present occasion, exceptionally, just for you."*)*

— WALT WHITMAN
Specimen Days

Texture

The mountain winds, like the dew and rain, sunshine and snow, are measured and bestowed with love on the forests to develop their strength and beauty. However restricted the scope of other forest influences, that of the winds is universal. The snow bends and trims the upper forests every winter, the lightning strikes a single tree here and there, while avalanches mow down thousands at a swoop as a gardener trims out a bed of flowers. But the winds go to every tree, fingering every leaf and branch and furrowed bole; not one is forgotten; the Mountain Pine towering with outstretched arms on the rugged buttresses of the icy peaks, the lowliest and most retiring tenant of the dells; they seek and find them all, caressing them tenderly, bending them in lusty exercise, stimulating their growth, plucking off a leaf or limb as required, or removing an entire tree or grove, now whispering and cooing through the branches like a sleepy child, now roaring like the ocean; the winds blessing the forests, the forests the winds, with ineffable beauty and harmony as the sure result.

— JOHN MUIR
"A Wind-Storm in the Forests"
from *The Mountains of California*

I GAVE MY HEART TO THE MOUNTAINS the minute I stood beside this river with its spray in my face and watched it thunder into foam, smooth to green glass over sunken rocks, shatter to foam again. I was fascinated by how it sped by and yet was always there; its roar shook both the earth and me.

When the sun dropped over the rim the shadows chilled sharply; evening lingered until foam on water was ghostly and luminous in the near-dark. Alders caught in the current sawed like things alive, and the noise was louder. It was rare and comforting to waken late and hear the undiminished shouting of water in the night. And at sunup it was still there, powerful and incessant, with the slant sun tangled in its rainbow spray, the grass blue with wetness, and the air heady as ether and scented with campfire smoke.

By such a river it is impossible to believe that one will ever be tired or old. Every sense applauds it. Taste it, feel its chill on the teeth: it is purity absolute. Watch its racing current, its steady renewal of force: it is transient and eternal. And listen again to its sounds: get far enough away so that the noise of falling tons of water does not stun the ears, and hear how much is going on underneath — a whole symphony of smaller sounds, hiss and splash and gurgle, the small talk of side channels, the whisper of blown and scattered spray gathering itself and beginning to flow again, secret and irresistible, among the wet rocks.

— WALLACE STEGNER
The Sound of Mountain Water
(Writing about Henry's Fork of the Snake River)

FOR MY OWN PART I am pleased enough with surfaces — in fact they alone seem to me to be of much importance. Such things for example as the grasp of a child's hand in your own, the flavor of an apple, the embrace of friend or lover, the silk of a girl's thigh, the sunlight on rock and leaves, the feel of music, the bark of a tree, the abrasion of granite and sand, the plunge of clear water into a pool, the face of the wind — what else is there? What else do we need?

— EDWARD ABBEY
Desert Solitaire

CHILDREN WANT TO TOUCH EVERYTHING, to smell the flowers, taste the leaves, dangle their feet in the water, pick apart the scat, carry home the bones. Sometimes I am impatient about this desire for direct contact. "Have respect!" I want to say. But in the end I hold my tongue, knowing they pay their respects by making sensual contact with the world. "The opposite of love," a friend reminds me, "is not hatred, but indifference."

— PAUL GRUCHOW
Grass Roots

AND WHEN LATER IN THE EVENING the owl sounds its soft, tremulous call, and small snaps and rustlings reveal the presence of other lives, the eyes have reached their proper limit. The sense we rely on above all others can never completely know the natural world, for nature's being is only partly what it shows. Its greater part, and greater beauty, is always past what human eyes can understand. When I started hiking desert canyons a few years ago, I kept hearing the song of a bird I couldn't see, a long descending series of sharply whistled notes. It was a canyon wren, I learned from the books, but what I learned from the bird was more important. It sang as I woke up, as brilliant sun spread down the great red walls, and it sang as I started farther up the twisting canyon, sloshing through pools and scrambling up dry water chutes, higher and deeper into the carving of time. And what I remember most vividly from those early hikes is no particular thing I saw, no one fern grotto or sandstone spire, no cottonwood or cactus garden. I remember a bird I couldn't see that called from around the next bend, from over the brink of a waterfall where the upper walls held the blaze of sky, where even as it steadily opened itself to sight, the canyon receded further and further into the depth of mystery.

— JOHN DANIEL
The Trail Home

CLOUDS OF MIST lie against the dark brow of timber. The nettling rain seems drawn against me. It drips from my face, wrinkles my hands, seeps down inside my boots, soaks my hair, runs down my neck, penetrates my heavy, sodden clothes. I lurk through the swaddling haze like a hunched gnome, leaning into an atmosphere so thick it seems less than half air. The only way to make the world any wetter is to submerge it completely. The muskeg is a slurry of soil and moss, steaming in the wet breath of dusk. Raindrops soak into the bark of drooping tree limbs, cling on the mesh of branchlets and twigs, and hang from the tips of needles. As soon as one falls, another immediately takes its place. A little deluge shakes down on me every time I brush a tree or shrub, but it no longer matters.

I could grumble about the rain and the discomfort, but after all, rain affirms what this country *is*. Today I stand face to face with the maker of it all, the source of its beauty and abundance, and I love the rain as desert people love the sun. I remember that the human body is ninety-eight percent water, and so, more than anything else, rain is the source of my own existence. I imagine myself transformed back to the rain from which I came. My hair is a wispy, wind-torn cloud. My eyes are rainwater ponds, glistening with tears. My mind is sometimes a clear pool, sometimes an impenetrable bank of fog. My heart is a thunderstorm, shot through with lightening and noise, pumping the flood of rainwater that surges inside my veins. My breath is the misty wind, whispering and soft one moment, laughing and raucous another. I am a man made of rain.

— RICHARD NELSON
The Island Within

FOR MANY YEARS, my walks have taken me down an old fencerow in a wooded hollow on what was once my grandfather's farm. A battered galvanized bucket is hanging on a fence post near the head of the hollow, and I never go by it without stopping to look inside. For what is going on in that bucket is the most momentous thing I know, the greatest miracle that I have ever heard of: it is making earth. The old bucket has hung there through many autumns, and the leaves have fallen around it and some have fallen into it. Rain and snow have fallen into it, and the fallen leaves have held the moisture and so have rotted. Nuts have fallen into it, or been carried into it by squirrels; mice and squirrels have eaten the meat of the nuts and left the shells; they and other animals have left their droppings; insects have flown into the bucket and died and decayed; birds have scratched in it and left their droppings or perhaps a feather or two. This slow work of growth and death, gravity and decay, which is the chief work of the world, has by now produced in the bottom of the bucket several inches of black humus. I look into that bucket with fascination because I am a farmer of sorts and an artist of sorts, and I recognize there an artistry and a farming far superior to mine, or to that of any human. I have seen the same process at work on the tops of boulders in a forest, and it has been at work immemorially over most of the land surface of the world. All creatures die into it, and they live by it.

— WENDELL BERRY
What Are People For?

THE EARTH CHANGES IN SPITE OF US, the way the watery atmosphere is changing even as I write, felt in the trees, understood in the waters, followed by birds. It is our medium. There is no substitute for the eternal weather.

A magnificent autumn wind, expressing a major exchange between warm fronts and cold, stirs the tall white pines into powerful expression. Timber-loaded, sinewy trunks wave in the wind, the upward curving, sweeping branches giving and dancing, nobly bending and bowing down, springing gracefully back again. Thus majesty leads to majesty. Some image also sleeps in trees. Do they not have a secret receptiveness, even if they cannot be said to see in an outright sense? Are they not a "seeing" response to the wind, this growing darkness and this waning light, as they are reflected in the motion and fiber of their being? While the wind roars, I put my ear to the trunk of a pine and hear the air hissing up and down, fairly crawling over that great column with its skin of rough bark, and it sounds like rushing water. It is part of an inheritance that we have been long neglecting, and to our peril.

— JOHN HAY
The Immortal Wilderness

WHATEVER THE REASON, I've found solace in living by water. Solace and a sense of humor restored. It amuses me to think that waterfront property rights ebb and flow with the tides. Today my property might extend well beyond my neighbor's buoy with a minus 2 low tide; tomorrow my property shrinks back to a plus 3 tide. It is water that shapes and defines my boundaries, not the other way round.

In learning to yield to water's having its way with us, we change our character. The Northwest Indians were not as warlike as the prairie or desert tribes. They were fisherman and whalers following the waters, not warriors claiming the land. Water, contrary to even our West's labyrinthian water laws, cannot be truly claimed. It's too malleable. Water may reflect us, mirror our deepest selves, but it won't bear our imprint, our scars. We can in a sense wound it through pollution and our contempt, but more often than not it will wash away those wounds over time.

Water leaves no trace of us, though over eons it has left its own mark in the whorls of canyon stone, wide-wandering tributaries, glacial melt. More than volcanic fire and wind, earth is sculpted by water. Perhaps, then, it is from water we can at last learn how to shape ourselves in its image.

— BRENDA PETERSON
Living by Water

THE EYE OF THE CORMORANT is emerald. The eye of the eagle is amber. The eye of the grebe is ruby. The eye of the ibis is sapphire. Four gemstones mirror the minds of birds, birds who mediate between heaven and earth.

We miss the eyes of birds, focusing only on feathers.

— TERRY TEMPEST WILLIAMS
Refuge

WHAT IS LIFE? we ask, knowing that the answer will come not as a headline but as an aggregate. Life is dewclaws and corsages and dust mites and alligator skin and feathers and whale's whiskers (as mammals, whales do have hair) and tree-frog serenades and foreskins and blue hydrangeas and banana slugs and war dances and cedar chips and bombardier beetles. Whenever we encounter something that is rare, we mentally add it to the seemingly endless list of forms that life can take. We smile in amazement as we discover yet another variation on an ancient theme. To hear the melody, we must hear all the notes.

— DIANE ACKERMAN
The Rarest of the Rare

THE FINEST QUALITY OF THIS STONE, these plants and animals, this desert landscape is the indifference manifest to our presence, our absence, our coming, our staying or our going. Whether we live or die is a matter of absolutely no concern whatsoever to the desert. Let men in their madness blast every city on earth into black rubble and envelope the entire planet in a cloud of lethal gas — the canyons and hills, the springs and rocks will still be here, the sunlight will filter through, water will form and warmth shall be upon the land and after sufficient time, no matter how long, somewhere, living things will emerge and join and stand once again, this time perhaps to take a different and better course. I have seen the place called Trinity, in New Mexico, where our wise men exploded the first atomic bomb and the heat of the blast fused sand into a greenish glass — already the grass has returned, and the cactus and the mesquite. On this bedrock of animal faith I take my stand, close by the old road that leads eventually out of the valley of paradox.

Yes. Feet on earth. Knock on wood. Touch stone. Good luck to all.

— EDWARD ABBEY
Desert Solitaire

VIEWED FROM THE DISTANCE OF THE MOON, the astonishing thing about the earth, catching the breath, is that it is alive. The photographs show the dry, pounded surface of the moon in the foreground, dead as an old bone. Aloft, floating free beneath the moist, gleaming membrane of bright blue sky, is the rising earth, the only exuberant thing in this part of the cosmos. If you could look long enough, you would see the swirling of the great drifts of white cloud, covering and uncovering the half-hidden masses of land. If you had been looking for a very long, geologic time, you could have seen the continents themselves in motion, drifting apart on their crustal plates, held afloat by the fire beneath. It has the organized, self-contained look of a live creature, full of information, marvelously skilled in handling the sun.

— LEWIS THOMAS
"The World's Biggest Membrane," from *The Lives of a Cell*

RAVENS SEEM LIKE ALMOST PHANTOM INDIVIDUALS, with a powerful ancestry. They tease me, in my rare meetings with them, toward recognition of a speech we have hardly begun to translate. I see ravens as my progenitors in spirit, birds of ill omen or good luck, all in one, of dark, mischievous minds, and of a sardonic pride. One flew quite close to me one day as I was standing next to a spruce tree on the Maine coast. It swished past me on stiff and silky feathers, carrying a mouse in its bill. I sensed enchantment in its character. The field guides fail to mention that. Perhaps we are afraid to stray too far beyond accepted nomenclature and the scientifically proven. We may sense too much of our suppressed anarchy to trust in merely intuitive equations, with their essences and vague parallels, but with the will to be haunted, I am leaving an open space for ravens. In any case, they got here first, and if they stand in with the sun and moon on intimate terms, as the Indians saw it, then they have lasting powers I ought at least to respect.

— JOHN HAY
The Immortal Wilderness

THE NIGHT BECAME VERY DARK. The rain surrounded the whole cabin with its enormous virginal myth, a whole world of meaning, of secrecy, of silence, of rumor. Think of it: all that speech pouring down, selling nothing, judging nobody, drenching the thick mulch of dead leaves, soaking the trees, filling the gullies and crannies of the wood with water, washing out the places where men have stripped the hillside! What a thing it is to sit absolutely alone, in the forest, at night, cherished by this wonderful, unintelligible, perfectly innocent speech, the most comforting speech in the world, the talk that rain makes by itself all over the ridges, and the talk of the water-courses everywhere in the hollows!

Nobody started it, nobody is going to stop it. It will talk as long as it wants, this rain. As long as it talks I am going to listen.

— THOMAS MERTON
"Rain and the Rhinoceros," from *Raids on the Unspeakable*

WINTER LOOKS LIKE A FICTIONAL PLACE, an elaborate simplicity, a Nabokovian invention of rarefied detail. Winds howl all night and day, pushing litters of storm fronts from the Beartooth to the Big Horn Mountains. When it lets up, the mountains disappear. The hayfield that runs east from my house ends in a curl of clouds that have fallen like sails luffing from sky to ground. Snow returns across the field to me, and the cows, dusted with white, look like snow-capped continents drifting.

The poet Seamus Heaney said that landscape is sacramental, to be read as text. Earth is instinct: perfect, irrational, semiotic. If I read winter right, it is a scroll — the white growing wider and wider like the sweep of an arm — and from it we gain a peripheral vision, a capacity for what Nabokov calls "those asides of spirit, those footnotes in the volume of life by which we know life and find it to be good."

— GRETEL EHRLICH
The Solace of Open Spaces

No landscape has more associations than grassland with the things humans have come to value most as they've spread through the colder parts of the earth: the sun as a celestial source of life, its useful earthly incarnation as fire, big herds of grazing animals. Since civilization began, successive waves of sun-worshiping, grassland nomads have dominated the human race, so that there probably is not a single system of belief without these grassland components. The human body itself seems as much an adaptation to grassland life as the hoofs of a bison. Erect gait, long legs, muscular buttocks, balancing arms, binocular vision — all are directed toward efficient movement in a landscape of horizons. If hominids hadn't left the forest, we would still be able to climb as well as apes.

If Eden often is imagined as a kind of arboretum, then heaven is seen as an equally green and flowery, but more open, place — a place where not even a fruit tree will obstruct the celestial light. Such an Elysian field has a striking likeness to an upland prairie in springtime, when herds are calving and winds smell of flowers. If a nomadic hunter or herder wanted a certain time protracted into eternity, it probably would be spring on a prairie.

— DAVID RAINS WALLACE
The Klamath Knot

So many disturbing traits, once you look into them.... sharks are the world's only known *intrauterine cannibals*; as eggs hatch within a uterus, the unborn young fight and devour each other until one well-adapted predator emerges. (If the womb is a battleground, what then the sea?) Also, without the gas-filled bladders that float other fish, sharks, if they stop swimming, sink. This explains their tendency to lurk along the bottom — twenty-one-foot, 4,600-pound benthic land mines with hundred year life-spans. Hard skin bristling with tiny teeth sheathes their flexible, cartilage skeletons — no bone at all. Conical snouts, black eyes without visible pupils, black-tipped pectoral fins. Tearing out and constantly being replaced, their serrated fangs have as many as twenty-eight stacked spares (a bite meter embedded in a slab of meat once measured a dusky shark's bite at eighteen tons per square inch). And all of the following have been found in shark bellies: a goat, a tomcat, three birds, a raincoat, overcoats, a car license plate, grass, tin cans, a cow's head, shoes, leggings, buttons, belts, hens, roosters, a nearly whole reindeer, even a headless human in a full suit of armor. Swimming with their mouths open, great whites are indiscriminate recyclers of the organic — my sensitive disposition, loving family and affection for life, my decent pickup, room full of books, preoccupation with chocolate in the afternoon and tendency to take things too personally: all immaterial to my status as protein.

— DANIEL DUANE
Caught Inside

49

EVOLUTION, OF COURSE, IS THE VEHICLE OF INTRICACY. The stability of simple forms is the sturdy base from which more complex stable forms might arise, forming in turn more complex forms, and so on. The stratified nature of this stability, like a house built on rock on rock on rock, performs, in Jacob Bronowski's terms, as the "ratchet" that prevents the whole shebang from "slipping back." Bring a feather into the house, and a piano; put a sculpture on the roof, sure, and fly banners from the lintels — the house will hold.

There are, for instance, two hundred twenty-eight separate and distinct muscles in the head of an ordinary caterpillar. Again, of an ostracod, a common fresh-water crustacean of the sort I crunch on by the thousands every time I set foot in Tinker Creek, I read, "There is one eye situated at the fore-end of the animal. The food canal lies just below the hinge, and around the mouth are the feathery feeding appendages which collect the food. . . . Behind them is a foot which is clawed and this is partly used for removing unwanted particles from the feeding appendages." Or again, there are, as I have said, six million leaves on a big elm. All right . . . but they are toothed, and the teeth themselves are toothed. How many notches and barbs is that to a world? In and out go the intricate leaf edges, and "don't nobody know why." All the theories botanists have devised to explain the functions of various leaf-shapes tumble under an avalanche of inconsistencies. They simply don't know, can't imagine.

— ANNIE DILLARD
Pilgrim at Tinker Creek

ONCE IN A LIFETIME, perhaps, one escapes the actual confines of the flesh. Once in a lifetime, if one is lucky, one so merges with sunlight and air and running water that whole eons, the eons that mountains and deserts know, might pass in a single afternoon without discomfort. The mind has sunk away into its beginnings among old roots and the obscure tricklings and movings that stir inanimate things. Like the charmed fairy circle into which a man once stepped, and upon emergence learned that the whole century had passed in a single night, one can never quite define this secret; but it has something to do, I am sure, with common water. Its substance reaches everywhere; it touches the past and prepares the future; it moves under the poles and wanders thinly in the heights of the air. It can assume forms of exquisite perfection in a snowflake, or strip the living to a single shining bone cast up by the sea.

— LOREN EISELEY
The Immense Journey

THE EVOCATION OF THE ECOZOIC ERA requires an entrancement within the world of nature in its awesome presence: whether in the Himalayan mountains or the Maine seacoast, the Pacific islands, the Sahara desert, the Greenland glacier, the Amazon rainforests, the Arctic snowfields, the prairies of mid-America, or any of the other fantastic presentations that nature makes of itself wherever we look. We need the expansive Earth, the distant sky, the flowering plants and trees and all that multitude of living forms about us; butterflies and bluebirds, Siberian tigers and tropical chimpanzees, dolphins and sea otters and the great blue whale. We know of no other place in the universe with such gorgeous self-expression as exists on Earth. This exuberance of life we see especially in the tropical rainforest with its unnumbered species of flowering plants and colorful insects and the full spectrum of living creatures of every kind. While everything exists for everything else we can only surmise the diminishment of the human mind and imagination if we did not have such magnificence in the natural phenomena about us.

— BRIAN SWIMME & THOMAS BERRY
The Universe Story

I AM OBSESSED BY BACTERIA, not just my own and those of the horse chestnut tree in my backyard, but bacteria in general. We would not have nitrogen for the proteins of the biosphere without the nitrogen-fixing bacteria, most of them living like special tissues in the roots of legumes. We would never have decay; dead trees would simply lie there forever, and so would we, and nothing on earth would be recycled. We could not keep cows, for cattle cannot absorb their kind of food until their intestinal bacteria have worked it over, and for the same reason there would be no termites to cycle the wood; they are, literally, alive with bacteria. We would not have luminous fish for our aquariums, for the source of that spectacular light around their eyes is their private colonies of luminescent bacteria. And we would never have obtained oxygen to breathe, for all the oxygen in our air is exhaled for our use by the photosynthetic microbes in the upper waters of the seas and lakes, and in the leaves of forests.

— LEWIS THOMAS
The Fragile Species

ABOVE ME THE CLOUDS ROLL IN, unfurling and smoking billows in malignant violet, dense as wool. Most of the sky is lidded over but the sun remains clear halfway down the west, shining in under the storm. Overhead the clouds thicken, then crack and split with a roar like that of cannonballs tumbling down a marble staircase, their bellies open — open late to run now — and the rain comes down.

Comes down: not softly not gently, with no quality of mercy but like heavy water in buckets, raindrops like pellets splattering on the rock, knocking the berries off the junipers, plastering my shirt to my back, drumming on my hat like hailstones and running in a waterfall off the brim. . . .

For five minutes the deluge continues under the barrage of thunder and lightning, then trails off quickly, diminishing to a shower, to a sprinkling, to nothing at all. The clouds move off and rumble for a while in the distance. A fresh golden light breaks through and now in the east, over the turrets and domes, stands the rainbow sign, a double rainbow with one foot in the canyon of the Colorado and the other far north in Salt Wash. Beyond the rainbow and framed within it I can see jags of lightning still playing in the stormy sky over Castle Valley.

The afternoon sun falls lower; above the mountains and the ragged black clouds hangs the new moon, pale fragment of what is to come; in another hour, at sundown, Venus too will be there, planet of love, to glow bright as chromium down on the western sky. The desert storm is over and through the pure sweet pellucid air the cliff swallows and the nighthawks plunge and swerve, making cries of hunger and warning and — who knows? — maybe of exultation.

— EDWARD ABBEY
Desert Solitaire

ONE AFTERNOON ON THE SIUSLAW RIVER in the Coast Range of Oregon, in January, I hooked a steelhead, a sea-run trout, that told me, through the muscles of my hands and arms and shoulders, something of the nature of the thing I was calling "the Siuslaw River." Years ago I had stood under a pecan tree in Upson County, Georgia, idly eating the nuts, when slowly it occurred to me that these nuts would taste different from pecans growing somewhere up in South Carolina. I didn't need a sharp sense of taste to know this, only to pay attention at a level no one had ever told me was necessary. One November dawn long before the sun rose, I began a vigil at the Dumont Dunes in the Mojave Desert in California, which I kept until a few minutes after the sun broke the horizon. During that time I named to myself the colors by which the sky changed and by which the sand itself flowed like a rising tide through grays and silvers and blues into yellows, pinks, washed duns, and fallow beiges.

It is through the power of observation, the gifts of eye and ear, of tongue and nose and finger, that a place first rises up in our mind; afterwards it is memory that carries the place, that allows it to grow in depth and complexity. For as long as our records go back, we have held these two things dear, landscape and memory. Each infuses us with a different kind of life. The one feeds us, figuratively and literally. The other protects us from lies and tyranny. To keep landscapes intact and the memory of them, our history in them, alive, seems as imperative a task in modern time as finding the extent to which individual expression can be accommodated, before it threatens to destroy the fabric of society.

— BARRY LOPEZ
The American Geographies

ON NEW YEAR'S DAY IN 1610, the astronomer Johannes Kepler presented his patron, John Wacker, Counsellor to the Imperial Court, a little book entitled *The Six-Cornered Snowflake*. It was a New Year's gift. It was also the first recorded step toward a mathematical theory of natural form.

Why, asks Kepler in his little treatise, do snowflakes fall as six-cornered starlets, "tufted like feathers"? There must be a *cause*, he asserts, for if it happens by chance, then why don't snowflakes fall with five corners or with seven? Casting about for an answer, Kepler considers other hexagons in nature: the shape of the cell in a honeycomb, for example. He shows that a hexagonal architecture for the honeycomb exactly suits the bee's purpose, for (as Kepler proves) the hexagon is the geometrical figure that enables the bee to enclose a maximum volume of honey with a minimum of wax. (It is a matter of the ratios of the areas of plane geometric figures to their perimeters and the sharing of sides between space-filling polygons, mathematical problems that Kepler found easy to solve.) Next Kepler considers the seeds of the pomegranate, which are also hexagonal in form. He demonstrates that this is the shape any round, pliable object will take if a mass of such objects is squeezed equally from every side into a minimal volume, as the seeds of the pomegranate are squeezed together in the growing fruit. . . . Then

Kepler reviews other possible "causes" for the snowflake's six-sided elegance: formal causes, teleological causes, efficient causes. He considers the role of beauty, function, and necessity. Perhaps, Kepler muses somewhat whimsically, like Olympian athletes snowflakes take care "not to fall in an ugly or immodest fashion." Or maybe, he concludes, in making snowflakes, nature simply "plays."

— CHET RAYMO
Honey from Stone

STEAM RISING. Water boiling. Geysers surging. Mud pots gurgling. Herds breathing. Hooves stampeding. Wings flocking. Sky darkening. Clouds gathering. Rain falling. Rivers surging. Lakes rising. Lightening striking. Trees burning. Thunder clapping. Smoke clearing. Eyes staring.

We call it a name — and the land calls back.

Yellowstone.

Echo system.

Echo.

— TERRY TEMPEST WILLIAMS
"Yellowstone: The Erotics of Place," from *An Unspoken Hunger*

WOLVES HAVE MARVELOUS LEGS. The first thing one notices about them is how high they are set on their skinny legs, and the instant, blurred gait these can switch into, bicycling away, carrying them as much as forty miles in a day. With brindled coats in smoky shades, brushy tails, light-filled eyes, intense sharp faces which are more focused than an intelligent dog's but also less various, they are electric on first sighting, bending that bushy head around to look back as they run. In captivity when they are quarreling in a cage, the snarls sound guttural and their jaws chop, but scientists watching pet wolves in the woods speak of their flowing joy, of such a delight in running that they melt into the woods like sunlight, like running water.

— EDWARD HOAGLAND
Heart's Desire

THEY SAY NOT TO ANTHROPOMORPHIZE — not to think of them as having feelings, not to think of them as being able to think — but late at night I like to imagine that they are killing: that another deer has gone down in a tangle of legs, tackled in deep snow; and that, once again, the wolves are feeding. That they have saved themselves, once again. That the deer or moose calf, or young dumb elk is still warm (steam rising from the belly as that part which contains the entrails is opened first), is now dead, or dying.

They eat everything, when they kill, even the snow that soaks up the blood.

This all goes on usually at night. They catch their prey from behind, often, but also by the nose, the face, the neck — whatever they can dart in and grab without being kicked. When the prey pauses, or buckles, it's over; the prey's hindquarters, or neck, might be torn out, and in that manner, the prey flounders. The wolves swarm it, then. They don't have thumbs. All they've got is teeth, long legs, and — I have to say this — great hearts.

— RICK BASS
The Ninemile Wolves

SMELLS ARE HARD TO DESCRIBE because we can't really remember them as we do sights and sounds, we can only recognize them. Smells lie deeper than our remembering, thinking neocortex, in the olfactory lobe we inherited from the early vertebrates. Yet smells are related to thought in profound ways because our nocturnal ancestors, the early mammals, lived by smell. The human ability to relate present to past and future may stem from their scent-tracking of food, an activity which takes place in time as well as space, unlike a hawk's immediate striking on sight, and thus implies planning. The curious resonance the olfactory senses have in memory, as when Proust tasted an epoch in a teacake, suggests that we have a great deal to learn from them.

— DAVID RAINS WALLACE
Bulow Hammock

I BEND OVER, looking at the debris caught there in the clear, black depth of the ice: I see a few small sticks, and many leaves. There are alder leaves, roughly toothed and still half green; the more delicate birch leaves and aspen leaves, the big, smooth poplar leaves, and narrow leaves from the willows. They are massed or scattered, as they fell quietly or as the wind blew them into the freezing water. Some of them are still fresh in color, glowing yellow and orange; others are mottled with grey and brown. A few older leaves lie sunken and black on the silty bottom. Here and there a pebble of quartz is gleaming. But nothing moves there. It is a still, cold world, something like night, with its own fixed planets and stars.

— JOHN HAINES
The Snow, the Stars, the Fire

FORM IS CERTAINTY. All nature knows this, and we have no greater adviser. Clouds have forms, porous and shape-shifting, bumptious, fleecy. They are what clouds need to be, to be clouds. See a flock of them come, on the sled of the wind, all kneeling above the blue sea. And in the blue water, see the dolphin built to leap, the sea mouse skittering, see the ropy kelp with its air-filled bladders tugging it upward; see the albatross floating day after day on its three-jointed wings. Each form sets a tone, enables a destiny, strikes a note in the universe unlike any other. How can we ever stop looking? How can we ever turn away?

— MARY OLIVER
Blue Pastures

THE LESSON OF A TREE

... I should not take either the biggest or the most picturesque tree to illustrate it. Here is one of my favorites now before me, a fine yellow poplar, quite straight, perhaps 90 feet high, and four thick at the butt. How strong, vital, enduring! how dumbly eloquent! What suggestions of imperturbability and being, as against the human trait of mere seeming. Then the qualities, almost emotional, palpably artistic, heroic, of a tree; so innocent and harmless, yet so savage. It is, yet says nothing. How it rebukes by its tough and equable serenity all weathers, this gusty-temper'd little whiffet, man, that runs indoors at a mite of rain or snow. Science (or rather half-way science) scoffs at reminiscence of dryad and hamadryad, and of trees speaking. But, if they don't, they do as well as most speaking, writing, poetry, sermons — or rather they do a great deal better. I should say indeed that those old dryad-reminiscences are quite as true as any, and profounder than most reminiscences we get. ("Cut this out," as the quack mediciners say, and keep by you.) Go and sit in a grove or woods, with one or more of those voiceless companions, and read the foregoing, and think.

— WALT WHITMAN
Specimen Days

Practice

I certainly have found "good in everything" — in all natural processes and products — not the "good" of Sunday-school books, but the good of natural law and order, the good of that system of things out of which we came and which is the source of our health and strength. It is good that fire should burn, even if it consumes your house; it is good that force should crush, even if it crushes you; it is good that rain should fall, even if it destroys your crops and floods your land. Plagues and pestilences attest the constancy of natural law. They set us to cleaning our streets and houses and to readjusting our relations to outward nature. Only in a live universe could disease and death prevail. Death is a phase of life, a redistributing of the type. Decay is another kind of growth.

— JOHN BURROUGHS
Riverby

WHEN YOU CONSIDER SOMETHING LIKE DEATH, after which (there being no news flash to the contrary) we may well go out like a candle flame, then it probably doesn't matter if we try too hard, are awkward sometimes, care for one another too deeply, are excessively curious about nature, are too open to experience, enjoy a nonstop expense of the senses in an effort to know life intimately and lovingly. It probably doesn't matter if, while trying to be modest and eager watchers of life's many spectacles, we sometimes look clumsy or get dirty or ask stupid questions or reveal our ignorance or say the wrong thing or light up with wonder like the children we all are. It probably doesn't matter if a passerby sees us dipping a finger into the moist pouches of dozens of lady's slippers to find out what bugs tend to fall into them, and thinks us a bit eccentric. Or a neighbor, fetching her mail, sees us standing in the cold with our own letters in one hand and a seismically red autumn leaf in the other, its color hitting our sense like a blow from a stun gun, as we stand with a huge grin, too paralyzed by the intricately veined gaudiness of the leaf to move.

— DIANE ACKERMAN
A Natural History of the Senses

You New Yorkers will excuse me for missing my barred owls, ruffed grouse and snowshoe rabbits, my grosbeaks and deer. I love what you love too. In the city and in the country there is a simple, underlying basis to life which we forget almost daily: that life is good. We forget because losing it or wife, children, health, friends is so awfully painful, and because life is hard, but we know from our own experience as well as our expectations that it can and ought to be good, and is even *meant* to be good. Any careful study of living things, whether wolves, bears or man, reminds one of the same direct truth; also of the clarity of the fact that evolution itself is obviously not some process of drowning beings clutching at straws and climbing from suffering and travail and virtual expiration to tenuous, momentary survival. Rather, evolution has been a matter of days well-lived, chameleon strength, energy, zappy sex, sunshine stored up, inventiveness, competitiveness, and the whole fun of busy brain cells. Watch how a rabbit loves to run; watch him set scenting puzzles for the terrier behind him. Or a wolf's amusement at the anatomy of a deer. Tug, tug, he pulls out the long intestines: ah, Yorick, how *long* you are!

An acre of forest will absorb six tons of carbon dioxide in a year. Wordsworth walked an estimated 186,000 miles in his lifetime.

— EDWARD HOAGLAND
Red Wolves and Black Bears

LIFE IN THE WILD is not just eating berries in the sunlight. I like to imagine a "depth ecology" that would go to the dark side of nature — the ball of crunched bones in a scat, the feathers in the snow, the tales of insatiable appetite. Wild systems are in one elevated sense above criticism, but they can also be seen as irrational, moldy, cruel, parasitic. Jim Dodge told me how he had watched — with fascinated horror — Orcas methodically batter a Gray Whale to death in the Chukchi Sea. Life is not just a diurnal property of large interesting vertebrates; it is also nocturnal, anaerobic, cannibalistic, microscopic, digestive, fermentative: cooking away in the warm dark. Life is well maintained at a four-mile ocean depth, is waiting and sustained on a frozen rock wall, is clinging and nourished in hundred-degree desert temperatures. And there is a world of nature on the decay side, a world of beings who do rot and decay in the shade. Human beings have made much of purity and are repelled by blood, pollution, putrefaction. The other side of the "sacred" is the sight of your beloved in the underworld, dripping with maggots. Coyote, Orpheus, and Izanagi cannot help but look, and they lose her. Shame, grief, embarrassment, and fear are the anaerobic fuels of the dark imagination. The less familiar energies of the wild world, and their analogs in the imagination, have given us ecologies of the mind.

— GARY SNYDER
The Practice of the Wild

AGAIN I THINK OF THE ANIMALS, because of the myriad ways in which they have helped us since we first regarded each other differently. They offered us early models of rectitude and determination in adversity, which we put into stories. The grace of a moving animal, in some ineluctable way, kindles still in us a sense of imitation. They continue to produce for us a sense of the Other: to encounter a truly wild animal on its own ground is to know the defeat of thought, to feel reason overpowered. The animals have fed us; and the cultures of the great hunters particularly — the bears, the dogs, and the cats — have provided the central metaphors by which we have taken satisfaction in our ways and explained ourselves to strangers.

— BARRY LOPEZ
"The Passing Wisdom of Birds," from *Crossing Open Ground*

IT'S DANGEROUS TO THINK OF OURSELVES as loathsome creatures or as perversions in the natural world. We need to see ourselves as having a rightful place and to rediscover that rightful place. We take pictures of all kinds of natural scenes and often we try to avoid having a human being in them. A natural place with human habitation blended into it is beautiful, too. In our society, we force ourselves into a greater and greater distance from the natural world by creating parks and wilderness areas where our only role is to go in and look. And we call this loving it. We lavish tremendous concern and care on scenery but we ignore the ravaging of environments from which our lives are drawn.

RICHARD NELSON
In conversation with John White, from *Talking on the Water*

PERHAPS MAN HAS SOMETHING TO LEARN after all from fellow creatures without the ability to drive harpoons through living flesh, or poison with strontium the planetary winds. One is reminded of those watery blue vaults in which, as in some idyllic eternity, Herman Melville once saw the sperm whales nurse their young. And as Melville wrote of the sperm whale, so we might now paraphrase his words in speaking of the porpoise. "Genius in the porpoise? Has the porpoise ever written a book, spoken a speech? No, his great genius is declared in his doing nothing particular to prove it. It is declared in his pyramidical silence." If man had sacrificed his hands for flukes, the moral might run, he would still be a philosopher, but there would have been taken from him the devastating power to wreak his thought upon the body of the world. Instead he would have lived and wandered, like the porpoise, homeless across currents and winds and oceans, intelligent, but forever the lonely and curious observer of unknown wreckage falling through the blue light of eternity. This role would now be a deserved penitence for man. Perhaps such a transformation would bring him once more into that mood of childhood innocence in which he talked successfully to all things living but had no power and no urge to harm. It is worth at least a wistful thought that someday the porpoise may talk to us and we to him. It would break, perhaps, the long loneliness that has made man a frequent terror and abomination even to himself.

— LOREN EISELEY
The Star Thrower

WHEN THE ANIMATE POWERS THAT SURROUND US are suddenly construed as having less significance than ourselves, when the generative earth is abruptly defined as a determinate object devoid of its own sensations and feelings, then the sense of a wild and multiplicitous otherness (in relation to which human existence has always oriented itself) must migrate, either into a supersensory heaven beyond the natural world, or else into the human skull itself — the only allowable refuge, in this world, for what is ineffable and unfathomable.

But in genuinely oral, indigenous cultures, the sensuous world itself remains the dwelling place of the gods, of the numinous powers that can either sustain or extinguish human life. It is not by sending his awareness out beyond the natural world that the shaman makes contact with the purveyors of life and health, nor by journeying into his personal psyche; rather, it is by propelling his awareness laterally, outward into the depths of a landscape at once both sensuous and psychological, the living dream that we share with the soaring hawk, the spider, and the stone silently sprouting lichens on its coarse surface.

— DAVID ABRAM
The Spell of the Sensuous

GIVEN THE COMPLEXITY OF POLITICAL SYSTEMS that, on the one hand, are intertwined with each and, on the other hand, are embedded in even more complex ecosystems, we should retain a humility about efforts to construct socially just and environmentally sustainable societies. Through the lens of geologic and evolutionary time, we are here but for moments, and cannot be considered particularly important.

The overwhelming likelihood is that just and sustainable societies will remain elusive. What else could we surmise from history? Yet this ought not deter us from pursuing these goals. Perhaps with a deepened sense of humility we can view our participation in social movements more as Gandhi did, as experiments in truth, and perhaps we can see popular struggles as mutations within the planet's body politic that millennia from now may well have proven adaptive, yielding flourishing life on Earth. In the meantime, such an understanding could help us take ourselves a bit less seriously, celebrate the everyday miracles of life, and act with greater kindness to our comrades and adversaries. An environmental movement infused with such perspectives would be more creative, produce more effective political theater, and serve as a more powerful life force than if distracted by rage, simple answers, or utopian dreams.

— BRON TAYLOR
"Earth First! Fights Back," from *Terra Nova: Nature & Culture*

ANIMAL PLAY IS A REASONABLY COMMON PHENOMENON, at least among certain mammals, especially in the young of those species. Play activities — by definition — are any that serve no immediate biological function, and which therefore do not directly improve the animal's prospects for survival and reproduction. The corvids, according to expert testimony, are irrepressibly playful. In fact, they show the most complex play known to birds. Ravens play toss with themselves in the air, dropping and catching again a small twig. They lie on their backs and juggle objects (in one recorded case, a rubber ball) between beak and feet. They jostle each other sociably in a version of "king of the mountain" with no real territorial stakes. Crows are equally frivolous. They play a brand of rugby, wherein one crow picks up a white pebble or a bit of shell and flies from tree to tree, taking a friendly bashing from its buddies until it drops the token. And they have a comedy-acrobatic routine: allowing themselves to tip backward dizzily from a wire perch, holding a loose grip so as to hang upside down, spreading out both wings, then daringly letting go with one foot; finally, switching feet to let go with the other. Such shameless hot-dogging is usually performed for a small audience of other crows.

— DAVID QUAMMEN
"Has Success Spoiled the Crow?" from *Natural Acts*

THE WORLD OF LIFE, OF SPONTANEITY, the world of dawn and sunset and starlight, the world of soil and sunshine, of meadow and woodland, of hickory and oak and maple and hemlock and pineland forests, of wildlife dwelling around us, of the river and its well-being — all of this some of us are discovering for the first time as the integral community in which we live. Here we experience the reality and the values that evoke in us our deepest moments of reflection, our revelatory experience of the ultimate mystery of things. Here...we receive those larger intuitions that lead us to dance and sing, intuitions that activate our imaginative powers in their most creative functions. This, too, is what inspires our weddings, our home life, and our joy in our children. Even our deepest human sensitivities emerge from our region, our place, our specific habitat, for the earth does not give itself to us in a global sameness. It gives itself to us in arctic and tropical regions, in seashore and desert, in prairielands and woodlands, in mountains and valleys. Out of each a unique shaping of life takes place, a community, an integral community of all the geological as well as the biological and the human components. Each region is a single community so intimately related that any benefit or any injury is immediately experienced through the entire community.

— THOMAS BERRY
The Dream of the Earth

IT IS HARD TO EVEN BEGIN TO GAUGE how much a complication of possessions, the notions of "my and mine," stand between us and a true, clear, liberated way of seeing the world. To live lightly on the earth, to be aware and alive, to be free of egotism, to be in contact with plants and animals, starts with simple concrete acts. The inner principle is the insight that we are interdependent energy-fields of great potential wisdom and compassion — expressed in each person as a superb mind, a handsome and complex body, and the almost magical capacity of language. To these potentials and capacities, "owning things" can add nothing of authenticity. "Clad in the sky, with the earth for a pillow."

— GARY SNYDER
Turtle Island

IT TOOK HUNDREDS OF MILLIONS OF YEARS to produce the life that now inhabits the earth — eons of time in which that developing and evolving and diversifying life reached a state of adjustment and balance with its surroundings. The environment, rigorously shaping and directing the life it supported, contained elements that were hostile as well as supporting. Certain rocks gave out dangerous radiation; even within the light of the sun, from which all life draws its energy, there were short-wave radiations with power to injure. Given time — time not in years but in millennia — life adjusts, and a balance has been reached. For time is the essential ingredient; but in the modern world there is no time.

— RACHEL CARSON
Silent Spring

NATURE EATS NATURE, and we are no exception, so let us have rituals that remind us. Hunters like Richard Nelson and Paul Shepard are asking us to restore the sacramental feeling to the necessary killing that sustains life. And not only killing animals: carrots, wheat, cherries from the tree, are all killed that we may eat them. Maybe, if we were more ritualistic, more directly concrete about the killing that goes into daily eating, we might be less extravagantly mad in those other killings — the twenty thousand murders an adolescent will have watched on television, the Vietnam, Iraq, and Panama bombings, and so on. There is a horror with blood letting, and only the most serious and communal rituals can encompass this horror — like what goes on in surgery or when an animal is slaughtered and dressed for winter eating.

— JAMES HILLMAN
In conversation with John White, from *Talking on the Water*

FOR THE GREEN PREHUMAN EARTH is the mystery we were chosen to solve, a guide to the birthplace of our spirit, but it is slipping away. The way back seems harder every year. If there is danger in the human trajectory, it is not so much in the survival of our own species as in the fulfillment of the ultimate irony of organic evolution: that in the instant of achieving self-understanding through the mind of man, life has doomed its most beautiful creations. And thus humanity closes the door to its past.

— EDWARD O. WILSON
The Diversity of Life

AS THE EMERGING SCIENCE OF THE SACRED, ecology requires spiritual disciplines very different from those that flowed from the theology of the Middle Ages, the Reformation, and the Industrial Revolution. In our time, authentic spirituality needs to be rooted in the *ecological imperative: Life in such a way that all future generations can enjoy as much or more biodiversity as we have enjoyed.* All else is self-serving delusion. Any form of spirituality that focuses exclusively on individual well-being and prosperity *is the dis-ease* for which it pretends to be the cure. Traditional religion agreed in identifying self-centeredness, greed, and delusion as the essence of hubris, sin, or maya. From the emerging ecospiritual perspective, *The Wall Street Journal* (the wisdom of this world) is foolishness. What could be more myopic and deluded than the belief that a worldwide marketplace economics can preserve the sacred bond that unites human and nonhuman life?

— SAM KEEN
Hymns to an Unknown God

IN THE END, I UNDERSTAND PERFECTLY WELL that defiance may mean prosperity and a sort of security — that more dams will help the people of Phoenix, and that genetic engineering will help the sick, and that there is so much progress that can still be made against human misery. And I have no great desire to limit my way of life. If I thought we could put off the decision, foist it on our grandchildren, I'd be willing. As it is, I have no plans to live in a cave, or even an unheated cabin. If it took ten thousand years to get where we are, it will take a few generations to climb back down. But this could be the epoch when people decide at least to go no further down the path we've been following — when we make not only the necessary technological adjustments to preserve the world from overheating but also the necessary mental adjustments to ensure that we'll never again put our good ahead of everything else's. This is the path I choose, for it offers at least a shred of hope for a living, eternal, meaningful world.

— BILL MCKIBBEN
The End of Nature

INNOCENCE SEES THAT THIS IS IT, and finds it world enough, and time. Innocence is not the prerogative of infants and puppies, and far less of mountains and fixed stars, which have no prerogatives at all. It is not lost to us; the world is a better place than that. Like any other of the spirit's good gifts, it is there if you want it, free for the asking, as has been stressed by stronger words than mine. It is possible to pursue innocence as hounds pursue hares: single-mindedly, driven by a kind of love, crashing over creeks, keening and lost in fields and forests, circling, vaulting over hedges and hills wide-eyed, giving loud tongue all unawares to the deepest, most incomprehensible longing, a root-flame in the heart, and that warbling chorus resounding back from the mountains, hurling itself from ridge to ridge over the valley, now faint, now clear, ringing the air through which the hounds tear, open-mouthed, the echoes of their own wails dimly knocking in their lungs.

— ANNIE DILLARD
Pilgrim at Tinker Creek

THE LESSONS WE LEARN FROM THE WILD become the etiquette of freedom. We can enjoy our humanity with its flashy brains and sexual buzz, its social cravings and stubborn tantrums, and take ourselves as no more and no less than another being in the Big Watershed. We can accept each other all as barefoot equals sleeping on the same ground. We can give up hoping to be eternal and quit fighting dirt. We can chase off mosquitoes and fence out varmints without hating them. No expectations, alert and sufficient, grateful and careful, generous and direct. A calm and clarity attend us in the moment we are wiping the grease off our hands between tasks and glancing up at the passing clouds. Another joy is finally sitting down to have coffee with a friend. The wild requires that we learn the terrain, nod to all the plants and animals and birds, ford the streams and cross the ridges, and tell a good story when we get back home.

— GARY SNYDER
The Practice of the Wild

IN SOME QUARTERS NOWADAYS it is fashionable to dismiss the balance of nature as a state of affairs that prevailed in an earlier, simpler world — a state that has now been so thoroughly upset that we might as well forget it. Some find this a convenient assumption, but as a chart for a course of action it is highly dangerous. The balance of nature is not the same today as in Pleistocene times, but it is still there: a complex, precise, and highly integrated system of relationships between living things which cannot safely be ignored any more than the law of gravity can be defied with impunity by a man perched on the edge of a cliff. The balance of nature is not a status quo; it is fluid, ever shifting, in a constant state of adjustment. Man, too, is part of this balance. Sometimes the balance is in his favor; sometimes — and all too often through his own activities — it is shifted to his disadvantage.

— RACHEL CARSON
Silent Spring

THE DIFFERENCE BETWEEN HUMANS and other organisms is that humans, having discerned something of how evolution works, are now able to confront their choices consciously. This is not the same as saying that we now can control evolution. I don't know how much of a difference it is in effect: we may be able to perceive our choices and still be unable to choose and act. By overpopulating the planet as we are now doing, for example, we are making an evolutionary choice just as unplanned as that of our hominid ancestors when they began cracking antelope and other hominids over the head with sticks. Nevertheless, we do differ from the first hominids in our having some notion of the implications of our behavior. In Biblical terms we have heeded the serpent, eaten of the tree of knowledge, and lost our innocence. We now must face the possibility of choosing between good and evil, or, in evolutionary terms, between survival and extinction.

— DAVID RAINS WALLACE
The Klamath Knot

PEOPLE HAVE TRADITIONALLY TURNED TO RITUAL to help them frame and acknowledge and ultimately even find joy in just such a paradox of being human — in the fact that so much of what we desire for our happiness and need for our survival comes at a heavy cost. We kill to eat, we cut down trees to build our homes, we exploit other people and the earth. Sacrifice — of nature, of the interests of others, even of our earlier selves — appears to be an inescapable part of our condition, the unavoidable price of all our achievements. A successful ritual is one that addresses both aspects of our predicament, recalling us to the shamefulness of our deeds at the same time it celebrates what the poet Frederick Turner calls "the beauty we have paid for with our shame." Without the double awareness pricked by such rituals, people are liable to find themselves either plundering the earth without restraint or descending into self-loathing and misanthropy. Perhaps it's not surprising that most of us today bring one of those attitudes or the other to our conduct in nature. For who can hold in his head at the same time a feeling of shame at the cutting down of a great oak, and a sense of pride at the achievement of a good building? It doesn't seem possible.

— MICHAEL POLLAN
A Place of My Own

To HARVEST ANY FOOD IS TO KILL LIVING BEINGS. This realization has become painful to us because of our lack of a philosophy of death as part of life and because in industrial societies we pay someone else to do the killing. Such a philosophy would include not only the moral necessity of killing, as the source of life, but recognition that we too are food. This continuity is basic to the whole of organic existence; the kinship of life requires it. Embalming, that civilized nicety pioneered by the ancient Egyptians and made law by us, is a desperate hope of escaping the cycle of bodily existence. Cremation is a half effort in the same direction.

In societies in which people individually kill their own food (be it the embryos in seeds or whole animals) there is no escape from the physical network; the perception, acknowledgment, and finally embrace of the hard truth as part of an affirmation of life. Thus the killing and eating of other beings is understood by most tribal peoples as part of a larger gift of life rather than a victory over nature or submission to a "bestial" nature. The individual hunter is not solely responsible, nor is she who tears the root from the ground or pulverizes the seeds more to blame than those who share the feast. Rites of celebration, purification, homage and veneration are groupwide. Virtually all religious concerns for these matters, among such peoples, bond death to both physical and spiritual renewal in some way or other.

— PAUL SHEPARD
The Only World We've Got

FOR SO LONG, THE STORY OF THE WEST has been that blood-scribing, that heartbeat of lighting out for "the territory" — the continental drift, westward toward freedom and liberty, as if some great magnetic store of it lies somewhere west of the Great Plains. But I sense that pulse may be — of necessity — finally changing and slowing, even reversing itself. I see more and more the human stories in the West becoming those not of passing through and drifting on, but of settling in and making a stand; and I think that there is a hunger for this kind of rhythm in towns, neighborhoods, and cities throughout the country — not just in rural areas, and not just in the West, but all over: that the blood-rhythms of wilderness which remain in us (as the old seas and oceans remain in us) are declaring, in response to the increasing instability of the outside forces that are working against us, the need for reconnection to rhythms that are stable and natural. And no matter whether those rhythms are found in a city, or in a garden, or in a relationship, or in the wilderness — it is the need and desire for them that we are recognizing and searching for, and I can feel it, the notion that settling-in and stand-making is the way to achieve or rediscover these rhythms. I can sense a turning-away from the idea, once pulsing in our own blood, that drifting or running is the answer, perhaps because the rhythms we need are becoming so hard to find, out in the fragmented worlds of both nature and man.

We can find these rhythms within ourselves.

— RICK BASS
The Book of Yaak

BIOPHILIA, IF IT EXISTS, AND I BELIEVE IT EXISTS, is the innately emotional affiliation of human beings to other living organisms....

Were there no evidence of biophilia at all, the hypothesis of its existence would still be compelled by pure evolutionary logic. The reason is that human history did not begin a mere 8,000 or 10,000 years ago, with the invention of agriculture and villages. It began hundreds of thousands or millions of years ago, with the origin of the genus *Homo*. For more than 99 percent of human history people have lived in hunter-gatherer bands intimately involved with other organisms. During this period of deep history, and still farther back, into paleohominid times, they depended on an exact learned knowledge of crucial aspects of natural history. That much is true even of chimpanzees today, who use primitive tools and have a practical knowledge of plants and animals. As language and culture expanded, humans also used living organisms of diverse kinds as a principal source of metaphor and myth. In short, the brain evolved in a biocentric world, not a machine-regulated one. It would therefore be quite extraordinary to find that all learning rules related to that world had been erased in a few thousand years, even in the tiny minority of humans who have existed for more than one or two generations in wholly urban environments.

— EDWARD O. WILSON,
"Biophilia and the Environmental Ethic"
from *In Search of Nature*

THE NATURE OF THE PRIMITIVE WORLD is at the center of our dilemma about essence, appearance, and change. Since we are not now what we once were — we are not bacteria or quadruped mammals, or apish hominids, or primitive people living without domesticated plants and animals — the dichotomy is clear enough. We each know as adults that we are no longer a child, yet we are not so sure that our being doesn't still embrace that other self who we were. We are attached to that primitive way of understanding, of double being, in spite of our modern perspective. Depth psychology has led us to understand that this going back is going into ourselves, into what, from the civilized historical view, is a "heart of darkness." Clearly a threat of the loss of self-identity is implied, swallowed by a second nature which is hidden and unpredictable.

As born anti-historians, our secret desire is to explicate the inexplicable, to recover that which is said to be denied. It is a yearning, a nostalgia in the bone, an intuition of the self as other selves, perhaps other animals, a shadow of something significant that haunts us, a need for exemplary events as they occur in myth rather than History. If not a necessity, it is a hunger that can be suppressed and distanced. The experience of that past is in terms of something still lived with, like fire, that still draws us. We cannot explain it, but it is there, made fragile in our psyche and hearts, drowned perhaps in our logic, but unquenchable.

> — PAUL SHEPARD
> "A Post-Historic Primitivism"
> from *The Wilderness Condition*

THE CHIEF LESSON IS THAT THE WORLD displays a lovely order, an order comforting in its intricacy. And the most appealing part of this harmony, perhaps, is its permanence — the sense that we are part of something with roots stretching back nearly forever, and branches reaching forward just as far. Purely human life provides only a partial fulfillment of this desire for a kind of immortality. As individuals, we can feel desperately alone: we may not have children, or we may not care much for how they have turned out; we may not care to trace ourselves back through our parents; some of us may even be general misanthropes, or feel that our lives are unimportant, brief, and hurried rushes toward a final emptiness. But the earth and all its processes — the sun growing plants, flesh feeding on these plants, flesh decaying to nourish more plants, to name just one cycle — gives us some sense of a more enduring role. The poet Robinson Jeffers, a deeply pessimistic man with regard to the human condition, once wrote, "The parts change and pass, or die, people and races and rocks and stars; none of them seems to me important in itself, but only the whole.... It seems to me that this whole alone is worthy of a deeper sort of love; and that there is peace, freedom, I might say a kind of salvation...."

— BILL MCKIBBEN
The End of Nature

IN AMERICA LATELY, we have been carrying on two parallel conversations: one about respecting human diversity, the other about preserving natural diversity. Unless we merge those two conversations, both will be futile. Our effort to honor human differences cannot succeed apart from our effort to honor the buzzing, blooming, bewildering variety of life on earth. All life rises from the same source, and so does all fellow feeling, whether the fellows move on two legs or four, on scaly bellies or feathered wings. If we care only for human needs, we betray the land; if we care only for the earth and its wild offspring, we betray our own kind. The profusion of creatures and cultures is the most remarkable fact about our planet, and the study and stewardship of that profusion seems to me our fundamental task....

Accounts of wilderness sojourns, like the sojourns themselves, often turn their backs on the human realm. Here is pristine nature, these accounts imply, and over there is corrupt society. Likewise, many who write about social problems, about poverty or prejudice or war, turn their backs on nature, as though we were acting out our destiny on a bare stage. But the stage is crowded with life, the stage is teeming — indeed, the stage is the main story. The only durable community is the one that embraces the whole planet, wild and tame....

At any rate, that is what I am trying to find, a way of writing and thinking about the whole of life, human as well as nonhuman, in all its dazzling array. Although I am caught much of the time in ego's shiny jar, distracted by my own reflections, there were moments during our wilderness sojourn when I slipped out of that small self and entered, however briefly, into the great community. Those are the moments worth telling.

— SCOTT RUSSELL SANDERS
Voyageurs

CAUGHT UP IN A MASS OF ABSTRACTIONS, our attention hypnotized by a host of human-made technologies that only reflect us back to ourselves, it is all too easy for us to forget our carnal inherence in a more-than-human matrix of sensations and sensibilities. Our bodies have formed themselves in delicate reciprocity with the manifold textures, sounds, and shapes of an animate earth — our eyes have evolved in subtle interaction with *other* eyes, as our ears are attuned by their very structure to the howling of wolves and the honking of geese. To shut ourselves off from these other voices, to continue by our lifestyles to condemn these other sensibilities to the oblivion of extinction, is to rob our own senses of their integrity, and to rob our minds of their coherence. We are human only in contact, and conviviality, with what is not human.

— DAVID ABRAM
The Spell of the Sensuous

EACH SPECIES IS THE PRODUCT OF MUTATIONS and recombinations too complex to be grasped by unaided intuition. It was sculpted and burnished by an astronomical number of events in natural selection, which killed off or otherwise blocked from reproduction the vast majority of its member organisms before they completed their lifespans. Viewed from the perspective of evolutionary time, all other species are our distant kin because we share a remote ancestry. We still use a common vocabulary, the nucleic-acid code, even through it has been sorted into radically different hereditary languages.

Such is the ultimate and cryptic truth of every kind of organism, large and small, every bug and weed. The flower in the crannied wall — it *is* a miracle. If not in the way Tennyson, the Victorian romantic, bespoke the portent of full knowledge (by which "I should know what God and man is"), then certainly a consequence of all we understand from modern biology. Every kind of organism has reached this moment in time by threading one needle after another, throwing up brilliant artifices to survive and reproduce against nearly impossible odds.

Organisms are all the more remarkable in combination. Pull out the flower from its crannied retreat, shake the soil from the roots into the cupped hand, magnify it for close examination. The black earth is alive with a riot of algae, fungi, nematodes, mites, springtails, enchytraeid worms, thousands of species of bacteria. The handful may be only a tiny fragment of one ecosystem, but because of the genetic codes of its residents it holds more order than can be found on the surfaces of all the planets combined. It is a sample of the living force that runs the earth — and will continue to do so with or without us.

— EDWARD O. WILSON
The Diversity of Life

FOR MOST OF MY LIFE, I have lived within range of the sea. Out of it in the springtime comes the alewife, the migratory species that swims inland to spawn in freshwater and then returns to where it came from. The alewife's large, lidless eyes, on both sides of its head, seem to offer messages from a depth I am unable to conceive of. That we may be able to dissect the structural properties of a fish's eyes, and to explore the depths of the ocean, does not mean we know these things. The great, unseen ranges are still beyond us. We have not yet discovered America.

— JOHN HAY
A Beginner's Faith in Things Unseen

"I THINK I COULD TURN AND LIVE WITH ANIMALS, they are so placid and self-contain'd," wrote Walt Whitman, "I stand and look at them long and long." It's from "Song of Myself," of course, that great epic hug bestowed on mid-nineteenth century America by our crazy-wild poet of inclusiveness and enthusiasm. The full section is worth remembering:

I think I could turn and live with animals, they are so
    placid and self-contain'd,
I stand and look at them long and long.

They do not sweat and whine about their condition,
They do not lie awake in the dark and weep for their sins,
They do not make me sick discussing their duty to God,
Not one is dissatisfied, not one is demented with the mania
    of owning things,
Not one kneels to another, nor to his kind that lived
    thousands of years ago,
Not one is respectable or unhappy over the whole earth.

Walt Whitman never met a snake or a sea cucumber that he didn't like, and this Whitmanesque attitude toward nature is exactly the one that seems to me exemplary. It is highly unscientific, it tends toward anthropomorphism, but then scientific objectivity and abstention from the anthropomorphic metaphor are not absolute virtues; those two forms of cold intellectual purity can help us understand nature, sure, but they shouldn't necessarily define our relations with it. The Whitman view is more inclusive, more daring, and ultimately more salubrious for all concerned. Few of us lesser souls, though, are fully capable of it. Some of us come to the sticking point over spiders, some over grizzly bears, some over rattlesnakes, or cocker spaniels, or house cats. But we can try.

— DAVID QUAMMEN
The Flight of the Iguana

THE HUMAN BODY DOES NOT MERELY RESEMBLE nature in its parts, it recapitulates the history of life, as much a living reenactment of evolutionary dramas as the Klamath Mountains. Corpuscles float in a primal nutrient bath of blood; intestines crawl about absorbing food in the manner of primitive worms; lungs absorb and excrete gases as do gills and leaves. No human organ would look out of place if planted in some Paleozoic sponge bed or coral reef. Even our brain is an evolutionary onion, the core we share with fish and reptiles, the secondary layer we share with other mammals, and the outer layer we share with other primates.

— DAVID RAINS WALLACE ✓
The Klamath Knot

FINALLY, I FIND MYSELF ASKING, what is nature? And the answer that comes back to me is this: It is our experience of a consciousness in the world itself, uncircumscribed by conventional thought, liberated as Frederick Turner puts it, from "the vicious circle of expectations governing perceptions which in turn confirm expectations." It is Blake's "seeing through, not with, the eyes." It is not merely a place relatively undominated by human influence, though it may be that too. We may take ourselves to the wildest reaches of the Brooks Range, but if we don't leave our everyday concerns behind, our concerns, and not the Brooks Range, are what we will experience....

Often when I walk out from my house into the hills surrounding it, I discover after twenty minutes or so that I have taken the house with me, have taken the unanswered letters and telephone calls, the windows that need caulking, the slights I suffered last week, the things I should have said but didn't, the things I plan to say next week but probably won't. My feet have been taking a walk without me. Every step has been clouded by the metronome beat of "yes, no, yes, no." Words like *ground squirrel*, *cinquefoil*, *osprey*, and *dove* flit across my consciousness in response to beings that appear, but I don't see them. It doesn't matter whether the ground I'm walking over is planted alfalfa or wild knapweed, whether the trees are virgin or second growth. If I am not aware of them, not conscious of their consciousness, nature doesn't exist for me, though I may be walking in Tierra del Fuego.

Nature is the great emptiness, the source, out of which our culture and all its flowering comes, and in order not to lose sight of this, not to become orphans lost in the minutiae of our daily lives and, like the rich man's son starving outside his father's gate, to forget who we are, it is vital that wildness be preserved for its own sake, which is to say, for our sake.

— DAN GERBER
"Walking in Tierra del Fuego," from *Sacred Trusts*

WE CANNOT FIND OUR LIVES IN WEIGHTS and measures. Microscopes and telescopes increase our context, they do not find origins or conclusions. Like the spirit we brought to this land, they probe, they examine, they explore. "Meaning," they proclaim, "is beyond our vision. Truth is below our sight."

But there is research of a different sort. It does not move, it does not seek. It watches until stillness shifts or silence makes a sound. It drinks in a universe whose origin and every manifestation is alive, and whose every movement demonstrates its laws. That which exists beyond our boundaries is not unknown, it is simply not revealed.

— KENT NERBURN
A Haunting Reverence

FRITJOF CAPRA WROTE: "Doing work that has to be done over and over again helps us to recognize the natural cycles of growth and decay, of birth and death, and thus become aware of the dynamic order of the universe." And it is true, in whatever we do, the brushing of hair, the cleaning of cages, we begin to see the larger order of things. In this place, there is a constant coming to terms with both the sacred place life occupies, and with death. Like one of those early physicians who discovered the strange, inner secrets of our human bodies, I'm filled with awe at the very presence of life, not just the birds, but a horse contained in its living fur, a dog alive and running. What a marvel it is, the fine shape life takes in all of us. It is equally marvelous that life is quickly turned back to the earth-colored ants and the soft white maggots that are time's best and closest companions. To sit with the eagles and their flute-like songs, listening to the longer flute of wind sweep through the lush grasslands, is to begin to know the natural laws that exist apart from our own written ones.

— LINDA HOGAN
"Waking Up the Rake," from *Dwellings*

Practice

I WONDER WHAT IT WOULD BE LIKE to go into a forest where nothing had name. If there were no word for tree stumps, would they sink into the duff? It's possible: After all, earth without form is void. And if we started over, giving names, would any fact about the forest compel us to name the same units? Would we label trees? Or instead would we find a name for the unity of roots and soil and microorganisms? Or would we label only the gloss of light on leaves and the shapes of shadows on the bark? How would we act in a forest if there were no names for anything smaller than an ecosystem? How could we walk, if there were no way to talk about anything larger than a cell?

All along the MacKenzie River Trail, there must be things we do not see, because they have no names. If we knew a word for the dark spaces between the pebbles on the river bottom, if we had a name for the nests of dried grass deposited by floods high in riverside trees, if there were a word apiece for the smell of pines in the sunshine and in the shadows, we would walk a different trail.

— KATHLEEN DEAN MOORE
Riverwalking

SCIENCE HASN'T UNDERMINED THE FEELING that God is present in the natural world — if anything, it's sharpened it, shown the scientists ever more sharply the limits of human understanding, continually increased their respect for the harmony around us....

Still, there is a way that science *has* helped to amputate our understanding of the world as a sacred place. Not through explanation — that only illuminates the real wonder. But inadvertently, through the inventions its findings make possible. New technologies have removed from most of us in the Western world any need to spend time in contact with the physical, and hence erased much of the chance to experience the divine in its grandest manifestations. Consider the car. When a scientist studies combustion, he peers through his instruments at one of the million aspects of the one great mystery. But when someone takes his findings and uses them to build a Pontiac, he helps to insulate us from those mysteries, from the contact with earth and air and water that comes with walking, or the communion with other life that is part and parcel of the horse and buggy. Through her telescope or her microscope or her oscilloscope the researcher sees the inevitable numinousness of the planet — science expands her vision. Through our windshields we see road signs and taillights — technology has blinkered us. Convenience always carries costs — this one may be worth paying, but it is high.

— BILL MCKIBBEN
The Age of Missing Information

Always my life comes up against the fact that it does not flourish or wane separate from worldwide experience, but is, in fact, wired, like a neuron in the brain, to all other circuits of life on earth.

This means that although at times I may flaunt my individuality, I do not exist independent of anything or anybody else. Sooner or later I am intimately affected by the death of a tiger in Burma, the grain prices on a Chicago commodities exchange, the birth of a cold front off the Aleutian Islands in Alaska. Wherever people congregate — in Paris, Bangor, or Beijing — their energy inevitably will lead to a demonstrable effect upon my being. We all are just as intricately wired into the processes of life. Most truly individual freedoms, for example, can be achieved only through a collective uprising. The more we admit this, the wider will be our concerns, the better chance we have to enhance our own well-being through our involvements with the sociology, economics, politics, and ecology of history.

Conscience, in other words, is collective.

Speaking of conscience, now that the spirit is willing, it's time for a discussion about the logistics of salvation.

The foundation of all my action, of course, is the understanding that any menace to any portion of the biosphere constitutes a personal threat against my own life.

Accepting that truth, no individual should have any qualms about the necessity for social commitment.

— JOHN NICHOLS
The Sky's the Limit

MORE THAN BEING IN CHURCH, I loved the junipers. There, I learned how ants move cookie crumbs and how the first drops of rain sound. I also learned to lie about the dirt on the knees of my pants.

In fourth grade we had an ant farm, one of those glass-paned horrors. Science class was rockets and beating the Russians. So I haunted the desert fringes after school and fled church picnics for the brush. I felt guilty as I slipped off, intent on my coyote education, but I didn't stop.

Cottonwood leaves sprouted, grew teeth, and rattled in the breeze. There were tadpoles in the seep, and then tiny frogs. When the leaves turned gold, the frogs went away. You could smell the rain before it fell, and the odors of juniper, piñon and sage were skeins of color, braided in the air.

My teachers stayed inside. My scout leaders lacked the names of plants. Instead, they gave orders: Chop wood, build a fire, string a monkey bridge. We'd find a spot and colonize it.

My forebears were farmers and ranchers, so being outdoors meant work. I bucked bales and herded sheep, and then joined the Forest Service. With Ed Abbey as my model, I scrubbed toilets, wrote tickets, and fought fires. It was good to sleep under canvas and spend whole days under the changing sky. A season of work paid for a quarter or two of school—shoved into hot rooms and stuffed with laws, axioms, chronologies, and procedures. It was a relief to take off for the next dead-end job. Education was the opposite of Outdoors.

But it shouldn't be. First, we need to roam, and learn from nature itself. To dabble, wade, dip, wallow, and splash. Toss pebbles, or pick them up. Sleep by the water until it sounds in our dreams. See our faces in a pool, and look beyond. Then, study hydrology.

— C.L. RAWLINS
"My Coyote Education," from *High Country News*

NO CULTURE HAS YET SOLVED the dilemma each has faced with the growth of the conscious mind: how to live a moral and compassionate existence when one is fully aware of the blood, the horror inherent in all life, when one finds darkness not only in one's own culture but within oneself. If there is a stage at which an individual life becomes truly adult, it must be when one grasps the irony in its unfolding and accepts responsibility for a life lived in the midst of such paradox. One must live in the middle of contradiction because if all contradiction were eliminated at once life would collapse. There are simply no answers to some of the great pressing questions. You continue to live them out, making your life a worthy expression of a leaning into the light.

— BARRY LOPEZ
Arctic Dreams

IN HIS FIRST SUMMERS, FORSAKING ALL HIS TOYS, my son would stand rapt for near an hour in his sandbox in the orchard, as doves and redwings came and went on the warm wind, the leaves dancing, the clouds flying, birdsong and sweet smell of privet and rose. The child was not observing; he was at rest in the very center of the universe, a part of things, unaware of ending and beginnings, still in unison with the primordial nature of creation, letting all light and phenomena pour through. Ecstasy is identity with all existence, and ecstasy showed in his bright paintings; like the Aurignacian hunter, who became the deer he drew on the cave wall, there was no "self" to separate him from the bird or flower. The same spontaneous identity with the object is achieved in the bold sumi painting of Japan — a strong expression of Zen culture, since to become one with whatever one does is a true realization of the Way.

Amazingly, we take for granted that instinct for survival, fear of death, must separate us from the happiness of pure and uninterpreted experience, in which body, mind, and nature are the same. And this debasement of our vision, the retreat from wonder, the backing away like lobsters from free-swimming life into safe crannies, the desperate instinct that our life passes unlived, is reflected in proliferation without joy, corrosive money rot, the gross befouling of the earth and air and water from which we came.

— PETER MATTHIESSEN
The Snow Leopard

I see the spectacle of morning from the hill-top over against my house, from day-break to sun-rise, with emotions which an angel might share. The long slender bars of cloud float like fishes in the sea of crimson light. From the earth, as a shore, I look out into that silent sea. I seem to partake its rapid transformations: the active enchantment reaches my dust, and I dilate and conspire with the morning wind. How does Nature deify us with a few and cheap elements! Give me health and a day, and I will make the pomp of emperors ridiculous. The dawn is my Assyria; the sun-set and moon-rise my Paphos, and unimaginable realms of faerie; broad noon shall be my England of the senses and the understanding; the night shall be my Germany of mystic philosophy and dreams.

— RALPH WALDO EMERSON
Nature

Belief

The original attitude of the American Indian toward the Eternal, the "Great Mystery" that surrounds and embraces us, was as simple as it was exalted. To him it was the supreme conception, bringing with it the fullest measure of joy and satisfaction possible in this life.

The worship of the "Great Mystery" was silent, solitary, free from all self-seeking. It was silent, because all speech is of necessity feeble and imperfect; therefore the souls of my ancestors ascended to God in wordless adoration. It was solitary, because they believed that He is nearer to us in solitude, and there were no priests authorized to come between a man and his Maker. None might exhort or confess or in any way meddle with the religious experience of another. Among us all men were created sons of God and stood erect, as conscious of their divinity. Our faith might not be formulated in creeds, nor forced upon any who were unwilling to receive it; hence there was no preaching, proselytizing, nor persecution, neither were there any scoffers or atheists.

— OHIYESA
(CHARLES ALEXANDER EASTMAN)
The Soul of an Indian

I'VE OFTEN THOUGHT of the forest as a living cathedral, but this might diminish what it truly is. If I have understood Koyukon teachings, the forest is not merely an expression or representation of sacredness, nor a place to invoke the sacred; the forest is sacredness itself. Nature is not merely created by God; nature *is* God. Whoever moves within the forest can partake directly of sacredness, experience sacredness with his entire body, breathe sacredness and contain it within himself, drink the sacred water as a living communion, bury his feet in sacredness, open his eyes and witness the burning beauty of sacredness. And when he cuts a tree from the forest, he participates in a sacred interchange that brings separate lives together.

The dark boughs reach out above me and encircle me like arms. I feel the assurance of being recognized, as if something powerful and protective is aware of my presence, looks in another direction but always has me in the corner of its eye. I am cautious and self-protective here, as anywhere, yet I believe that a covenant of mutual regard and responsibility binds me together with the forest. We share in a common nurturing. Each of us serves as an amulet to protect the other from inordinate harm. I am never alone in this wild forest, this forest of elders, this forest of eyes.

— RICHARD NELSON
The Island Within

MY NOTES TELL ME I have seen a thousand geese this fall. Every one of these in the course of their epic journey from the arctic to the gulf has on one occasion or another probably served man in some equivalent of paid entertainment. One flock perhaps has thrilled a score of schoolboys, and sent them scurrying home with tales of high adventure. Another, passing overhead of a dark night, has serenaded a whole city with goose music, and awakened who knows what questionings and memories and hopes. A third perhaps has given pause to some farmer at his plow, and brought new thoughts of far lands and journeyings and peoples, where before was only drudgery, barren of any thought at all. I am sure those thousand geese are paying human dividends on a dollar value. Worth in dollars is only an exchange value, like the sale value of a painting or the copyright of a poem. What about the replacement value? Supposing there were no longer any painting, or poetry, or goose music? It is a black thought to dwell upon, but it must be answered. In dire necessity somebody might write another *Iliad*, or paint an "Angelus," but fashion a goose?

— ALDO LEOPOLD
A Sand County Almanac

ON OUR SASKATCHEWAN PRAIRIE, the nearest neighbor was four miles away, and at night we saw only two lights on all the dark rounding earth. The earth was full of animals — field mice, ground squirrels, weasels, ferrets, badgers, coyotes, burrowing owls, snakes. I knew them as my little brothers, as fellow creatures, and I have never been able to look upon animals in any other way since. The sky in that country came clear down to the ground on every side, and it was full of great weathers, and clouds, and winds, and hawks. I hope I learned something from knowing intimately the creatures of the earth; I hope I learned something from looking a long way, from looking up, from being much alone. A prairie like that, one big enough to carry the eye clear to the sinking, rounding horizon, can be as lonely and grand and simple in its forms as the sea. It is as good a place as any for the wilderness experience to happen; the vanishing prairie is as worth preserving for the wilderness idea as the alpine forests.

— WALLACE STEGNER
"Coda: Wilderness Letter"
from *The Sound of Mountain Water*

IN MY JUDGEMENT, only when we perceive that the value of the living natural world is grounded in something greater than ourselves, in something other than our human ability to value it, will our rational capacities be satisfied fully that life on earth matters. This claim is compatible with many religious perceptions — monisms, polytheisms, monotheisms, pantheisms, polytheisms, animisms — it can withstand scrutiny whether there is a personal God, or if the divine is conceived as an impersonal cosmic presence, or if the land is inspirited with each earthly entity participating in and expressing the divine.

Even though I consider a religious worldview essential for a compelling environmental ethics — however — most days I am agnostic. Yet I also have deep, affective experiences of the value of people, of our earthy home, of our miraculous kindred relations. These experiences are meaningless in the absence of the sacred, and yet *they are as convincing as what I know scientifically*. In the final analysis we must choose — either to believe in a fascinating but meaningless universe — or in one congruent with our own experiences of the value of people and place.

Choosing is difficult. Yet, I am compelled by my own affective life, my aesthetic preferences, by a few moments in nature that are beyond words, to affirm that it all matters. I am not sure of much, but I am sure of this. I may not be a person fueled with an everyday mystical sense of unity with the universe, by contacts with nature-spirits — let alone by contacts with a pantheon or personal god that consecrates the earth through creative fiat. In my own quasi-agnostic way, I must *resolve* to believe in the sacred, because it makes good sense, because it coheres with my experience of the value that surrounds me, because when I am at my most perceptive, it rings true. I must also nurture this fragile conviction.

— BRON TAYLOR
"On Secular or Sacred Ground?"

WHATEVER EVALUATION WE FINALLY MAKE of a stretch of land, however, no matter how profound or accurate, we will find it inadequate. The land retains an identity of its own, still deeper and more subtle than we can know. Our obligation toward it then becomes simple: to approach with an uncalculating mind, with an attitude of regard. To try to sense the range and variety of its expression — its weather and colors and animals. To intend from the beginning to preserve some of the mystery within it as a kind of wisdom to be experienced, not questioned. And to be alert for its openings, for that moment when something sacred reveals itself within the mundane, and you know the land knows you are there.

— BARRY LOPEZ
Arctic Dreams

OUR INSTINCT FOR FAITH is like a well-bred Border collie, who, lacking cattle or sheep, will herd children or chickens or cats. If we don't direct our faith toward God or into some authentic "way" of the soul, then we direct it toward progress or science or weaponry or education or nature or human nature or doctors or gurus or genetic engineers or computers or NASA. And as we reduce the objects of our faith and so reduce our faith, we inevitably reduce ourselves. We are by nature creatures of faith, as perhaps all creatures are; we all live by counting on things that cannot be proved. As creatures of faith, we must choose either to be religious or to be superstitious, to believe in things that cannot be proved or to believe in things that can be disproved. The present age is an age of superstition, and some of our shallowest superstitions have the authorization of our hardest-headed rationalists and realists. The modern ambition to control nature, for instance, is an ambition based foursquare on a superstition: the idea that what we take nature to be is what nature is, or that nature is that to which it can be reduced. If nature is to be controlled, then it has to be reduced to that which is theoretically controllable. It must be understood as a machine or as the sum of its known, separable, and decipherable parts.

Care, on the contrary, rests upon genuine religion. Care allows creatures to escape our explanations into their actual presence and their essential mystery. In taking care of fellow creatures, we acknowledge that they are not ours; we acknowledge that they belong to an order and a harmony of which we ourselves are parts. To answer to the perpetual crisis of our presence in this abounding and dangerous world, we have only the perpetual obligation of care.

— WENDELL BERRY
Another Turn of the Crank

IF WE WERE TO CHOOSE A SINGLE EXPRESSION for the universe it might be "celebration," celebration of existence and life and consciousness, also of color and sound but especially in movement, in flight through the air and swimming through the sea, in mating rituals and care of the young. But then too there is the pathos of both living and dying, of consuming and being consumed. There is the vast hydrological cycle with its sequence of abundance and scarcity, its expression of the tragic as well as the delightful moments of temporal existence.

— BRIAN SWIMME & THOMAS BERRY
The Universe Story

THERE IS NO MORE USE IN CONQUEST; there are only new ways to connect. The first connection is very simple. It's a feeling that we are not alone, that history lives alongside our most ordinary comings and goings and that there are global as well as personal consequences from our actions, our dispossessions. If we harm, we will be harmed; this is not environmental karma, this is scientific fact. The natural world is our greater body. If we destroy the breathing rain forests, sooner or later we too will cease breathing. This bonding of or being with the Earth is not radical; we do it when we die by simply burying ourselves in the ground.

— BRENDA PETERSON
"Where the Green River Meets the Amazon"
from *Living by Water*

WE'LL NEVER AGAIN BE MEMBERS of the land as other animals are. We are daylight people, we live by the artifice of our kind. But we are animals too, born into a world of animals. We share the same sun, the same wind and rain, grass and trees, the same hospitable surface of this planet that became alive. Separate and together, we are born of mystery into mystery, expressions of a single miracle. It lives in the raccoon's quick paws and lively strength, in the bear's glance and the red squirrel gripping the limb, in the cries of the coyote, the gaze of the deer, the honeybee's dance. It swims in rivers and sea, flies on wings through the ocean of air, it stirs in the stillness of the forest night — it burns in the screech owl and it burns in me, the same fire, the same brief fire, shining from eyes to other eyes.

— JOHN DANIEL
The Trail Home

WE HAVE TROUBLE WHEN WE TRY TO UNDERSTAND the earth in terms of ourselves. Is it property? Does it belong to some absentee father? Perhaps not. But what is it to us? The golden mother in whose lap we buried our earliest faces? The heavy-breasted goddess, dancing with fists full of corpses, rattling a necklace of skulls?

I can't think of the earth as my mother. I have a real mother, a woman I love, who is equally flesh and spirit. She is neither large nor dangerous. I can think of the earth as a grandmother, perhaps, so massive and old and full of life that she's grown into remoteness: one of the oldest, unspeaking, who looks over the country of death and into life again.

But the metaphors clash. Can I be the steward of my grandmother's body? Only if she is weak, incompetent, addled. Or if she is chattel, something owned.

So maybe the earth is too big to love all at once, too great and various to be known by one word or image. I've seen the photograph taken from the moon of our jewelled island in a black sea. Yet at that scale, I can't see faces, can't hear voices, can't discern the landmarks of the place and time in which I live.

Can you love humanity? Can you love women without loving a woman? Can you love men without loving a man? Earth may be too great and various for what we call love, except as intention. There may be no meeting, no enactment, no consummation with the whole of it. When I was four, I knew a horse. All horses, horsekind, the *Horse*, I have yet to know.

We speak more easily of places and things: specific, singular, irreplaceable. This is the scale on which we live. To love the unknown is a ceaseless, bodiless hunger. The trick is to love what you know, what's familiar, what you've endured. To live with it, each day.

— C.L. RAWLINS
"Grandpa's Horse," from *Sacred Trusts*

I WOULD BE CONVERTED TO A RELIGION OF GRASS. *Sleep the winter away and rise headlong each spring. Sink deep roots. Conserve water. Respect and nourish your neighbors and never let trees gain the upper hand.* Such are the tenets and dogmas. As for practice — *grow lush in order to be devoured or caressed, stiffen in sweet elegance, invent startling seeds* — those also make sense. *Bow beneath the arm of fire. Connect underground. Provide. Provide. Be lovely and do no harm.*

— LOUISE ERDRICH
"Big Grass," from *Heart of the Land*

WE ARE GRACED BY THE EVENTS ON JUPITER. We were graced by the supernova explosion five-and-a-half billion years ago. We were graced by the fireball fourteen billion years ago, that set things going, that made stories possible. We are graced every day the sun comes up, and every day a tiger smiles at you, and every day a whale winks at us. We are graced constantly by nature! Grace is nature, and if we would get that right, we would be green again, because there is plenty of grace to go around. Don't let them fool you. There's plenty of grace to go around. It's our problem that we are not receptive to all the grace we are swimming in, day in and day out.

Kabir, the wonderful Eastern mystic, says, "I laugh at the fish in the water who tells me he is thirsty!" That's us folks! We are fish in water. We think we are thirsty for grace. The water is the divine light. We're breathing it in, and breathing it out, just like a fish. Wake up. "Wake up!" — as Kabir says — "You have been sleeping for hundreds of millions of years."

— MATTHEW FOX
"Bringing Nature and Grace Together Again"
from *The Soul Unearthed*

WE SHOULD BE CLEAR ABOUT WHAT HAPPENS when we destroy the living forms of this planet. The first consequence is that we destroy modes of divine presence. If we have a wonderful sense of the divine, it is because we live amid such awesome magnificence. If we have refinement of emotion and sensitivity, it is because of the delicacy, the fragrance, and indescribable beauty of song and music and rhythmic movement in the world about us. If we grow in our life vigor, it is because the earthly community challenges us, forces us to struggle to survive, but in the end reveals itself as a benign providence. But however benign, it must provide that absorbing drama of existence whereby we can experience the thrill of being alive in a fascinating and unending sequence of adventures.

If we have powers of imagination, these are activated by the magic display of color and sound, of form and movement, such as we observe in the clouds of the sky, the trees and bushes and flowers, the waters and the wind, the singing birds, and the movement of the great blue whale through the sea. If we have words with which to speak and think and commune, words for the inner experience of the divine, words for the intimacies of life, if we have words for telling stories to our children, words with which we can sing, it is again because of the impressions we have received from the variety of beings about us.

— THOMAS BERRY
The Dream of the Earth

ON SEVERAL OCCASIONS RECENTLY, I have been a recipient of an unmistakable grace. Shortly before dawn a couple of years ago, I was wakened by cat growls in a very low register. "Can't be our house cat," I thought. I went out to look but could find nothing. Next morning, the same thing occurred. The third morning, I crept out of bed, followed the sound of the bass fiddle cat music deep into the woods, and came upon two bobcats sitting at opposite ends of a log, growling a duet to either Mars or Aphrodite. I stood silently, waiting for the drama of either combat or love to begin. A timeless interval later, the concert ended and the singers disappeared silently into the semidarkness. I felt I had been an honored witness at a sacred ritual, blessed by the wild grace of beings whose beauty and mystery were not dependent on humankind. It is said that in ancient Greece in the Eleusinian mysteries, the climax of the ceremony of initiation was the moment when the initiate was shown a single ear of corn. Perhaps epiphanies are always like this: Something as ordinary as an ear of corn, bread and wine, or a bobcat suddenly becomes transparent to the creative source from whom all life, and blessings, flow.

— SAM KEEN
Hymns to an Unknown God

I THINK IT'S CICERO WHO SAYS that when you go into a great tall grove, the presence of a deity becomes known to you. There are sacred groves everywhere. Going into the forest as a little boy, I can remember worshiping a tree, a great big old tree, thinking, "My, my, what you've known and been." I think this sense of the presence of creation is a basic mood of man. But we live now in a city. It's all stone and rock, manufactured by human hands. It's a different kind of world to grow up in when you're out in the forest with the little chipmunks and the great owls. All these things are around you as presences, representing forces and powers and magical possibilities of life that are not yours and yet are all part of life, and that opens it out to you. Then you find it echoing in yourself, because you are nature. When a Sioux Indian would take the calumet, the pipe, he would hold it up stem to the sky so that the sun could take the first puff. And then he'd address the four directions always. In that frame of mind, when you're addressing yourself to the horizon, to the world that you're in, then you're in your place in the world. It's a different way to live.

— JOSEPH CAMPBELL
The Power of Myth

WHAT DISAPPEARS WITH A DEBASEMENT of wild landscapes is more than genetic diversity, more than a homeland for Henry Beston's "other nations," more, to be perfectly selfish, than a source of future medical cures for human illness or a chance for personal revitalization on a wilderness trip. We stand to lose the focus of our ideals. We stand to lose our sense of dignity, of compassion, even our sense of what we call God. The philosophy of nature we set aside eight thousand years ago in the Fertile Crescent we can, I think, locate again and greatly refine in North America. The New World is a landscape still overwhelming in the vigor of its animals and plants, resonant with mystery. It encourages, still, an enlightened response toward indigenous cultures that differ from our own, whether Aztecan, Lakotan, lupine, avian, or invertebrate. By broadening our sense of the intrinsic worth of life and by cultivating respect for other ways of moving toward perfection, we may find a sense of resolution we have been looking for, I think, for centuries.

— BARRY LOPEZ
"The Passing Wisdom of Birds"
from *Crossing Open Ground*

I LOOK DOWN AT THE SOIL UNDER MY FEET, layered with decaying alder leaves. Each fallen leaf eventually rots, transforms, and is shaped into other organisms, while the tree lives on. Each tree eventually falls, transforms, and is shaped into other organisms, while the forest lives on. The forest, too, will vanish and be transformed, shaped into other communities of organisms that will live on. How can there be a final, absolute death if life as a whole, or earth itself, is the organism?

What I've dreaded most about death is the prospect of *leaving*, of lapsing into a nothingness beyond life. But in this endless process of metamorphosis, there can be no final death, only a transmutation of life. A flowing through. A constantly changing participation in the living community. And the fate of all living things is an earthbound immortality. During these moments, a profound comfort spreads through me, as I look at the island, the forest, and the stream, realizing I can never be separated from them, can never be alone, can never fall away.

— RICHARD NELSON
The Island Within

A CHILD'S WORLD IS FRESH AND NEW and beautiful, full of wonder and excitement. It is our misfortune that for most of us that clear-eyed vision, that true instinct for what is beautiful and awe-inspiring, is dimmed and even lost before we reach adulthood. If I had influence with the good fairy who is supposed to preside over the christening of all children I should ask that her gift to each child in the world be a sense of wonder so indestructible that it would last throughout life, as an unfailing antidote against the boredom and disenchantment of later years, the sterile preoccupation with things that are artificial, the alienation from the sources of our strength.

What is the value of preserving and strengthening this sense of awe and wonder, this recognition of something beyond the boundaries of human existence? Is the exploration of the natural world just a pleasant way to pass the golden hours of childhood or is there something deeper?

I am sure there is something much deeper, something lasting and significant. Those who dwell, as scientists or laymen, among the beauties and mysteries of the earth are never alone or weary of life. Whatever the vexations or concerns of their personal lives, their thoughts can find paths that lead to inner contentment and to renewed excitement in living. Those who contemplate the beauty of the earth find reserves of strength that will endure as long as life lasts. There is symbolic as well as actual beauty in the migration of the birds, the ebb and flow of the tides, the folded bud ready for the spring. There is something infinitely healing in the repeated refrains of nature — the assurance that dawn comes after night, and spring after the winter.

— RACHEL CARSON
The Sense of Wonder

IF I CHOOSE NOT TO BECOME ATTACHED TO NOUNS — a person, place, or thing — then when I refuse an intimate's love or hoard my spirit, when a known landscape is bought, sold, and developed, chained or grazed to a stubble, or a hawk is shot and hung by its feet on a barbed-wire fence, my heart cannot be broken because I never risked giving it away.

But what kind of impoverishment is this to withhold emotion, to restrain our passionate nature in the face of a generous life just to appease our fears? A man or woman whose mind reins in the heart when the body sings desperately for connection can only expect more isolation and greater ecological disease. Our lack of intimacy with each other is in direct proportion to our lack of intimacy with the land. We have taken our love inside and abandoned the wild.

— TERRY TEMPEST WILLIAMS
"Winter Solstice at the Moab Slough"
from *An Unspoken Hunger*

I BELIEVE A SANER RELATION to the natural world must end our servitude to modernity by creating new practices that alter our daily routines. I also believe that no resolution to the crises facing the wild earth will achieve more than a modicum of success without an integration of spiritual practice into our lives. Any spiritual tradition worthy of the name teaches the diminishment of desire, and it is desire in all its forms — simple greed, avarice, hoarding, the will to power, the will to truth, the rush of population growth, the craving for control — that fuels the destruction of our once-fair planet. I believe that virtually all problems are problems of scale, and I know, to the degree that I know anything, that desire usually drives us to adopt scales that are inappropriate to their subjects. This is as true for emotion and forestry as it is for hunting and global economics.

— JACK TURNER
The Abstract Wild

WHAT VALUE HAS WILDLIFE from the standpoint of moral and religion? I heard of a boy once who was brought up an atheist. He changed his mind when he saw that there were a hundred-odd species of warblers, each bedecked like to the rainbow, and each performing yearly sundry thousands of miles of migration about which scientists wrote wisely but did not understand. No "fortuitous concourse of elements" working blindly through any number of millions of years could quite account for why warblers are so beautiful. No mechanistic theory, even bolstered by mutations, has ever quite answered for the colors of the cerulean warbler, or the vespers of the woodthrush, or the swansong, or — goose music. I dare say this boy's convictions would be harder to shake than those of many inductive theologians. There are yet many boys to be born who, like Isaiah, "may see, and know, and consider, and understand together, that the hand of the Lord hath done this." But where shall they see, and know, and consider? In museums?

— ALDO LEOPOLD
A Sand County Almanac

WITH EACH BREATH of the earth's atmospheric membrane I also inhale the breaths of millions of other human beings, animals, birds, fish, algae, you name it. And not just of those things and people alive today. Every second there mingles in me the exhaust of those who have lived, died, breathed, and altered their personal matter into the energy of the atmosphere throughout the ages of history... my origins.

Actually, who's to say of just exactly what this airy membrane consists? Ashes of cremated billions float forever above our heads, among the dust particles kicked up by horses on country roads and tattered flakes of old mosquito wings. We can analyze the various gases, the hydrogen, oxygen, helium; we can isolate the trace metals polluting our air; we can track down and accuse the acid rains distilled from clouds, yet are we approaching even a semidefinitive analysis? Natural gases on top of chemicals released by combustion engines may indeed account for the variety of blues, yellows, and dancing greens that perpetually glorify the oxygen protecting us from being pulverized into a cratered desert by that constant barrage of meteors falling victim to friction long before reaching our topsoil. Yet this envelope of life-granting ether may be charged with an altogether different energy, "a penumbral rainbow" Loren Eiseley once called it, "that cloud of ideas, visions, and institutions which hover about, indeed constitute human society, but which can be dissected from no single brain."

— JOHN NICHOLS
The Sky's the Limit

IN THE BOOK OF JOB, the beleaguered man cries out that all creatures, himself included, rest in the hand of God:

> *But ask the beasts, and they will teach you;*
> *the birds of the air, and they will tell you;*
> *or the plants of the earth, and they will teach you;*
> *and the fish of the sea will declare you.*

The key word here is *ask*. What the birds and beasts and countryside teach us depends on the questions we pose. A person wielding a fifty-ton digger in search of coal will learn quite different lessons from one who wields a pair of binoculars in search of warblers. Job assumed that anybody who listened to the creation would hear the whisper of the creator. But generally we hear what our ears have been prepared for, and if we do not go seeking divinity we are not likely to find it. In the long run and in a blunt manner, nature has its own say: species that poison or exhaust their habitat die out. But in the short run, nature does not declare how we should approach it; that lesson we learn from culture.

— SCOTT RUSSELL SANDERS
Tokens of Mystery

Q: WHAT DOES THE WORD *sacred* mean to you?

A: It's the relinking, the rediscovery, the reconnection of the little point of light, the sentience that you are, with the totality. On the one hand this sounds impossible, but on the other it has been uttered in 1001 different ways in 1001 different religious traditions.

If you are open, if you can somehow keep clear in your mind how much of your being has been socially defined, then you can continually slip through the cracks of that social definition and encounter the sacred. You can see the sacred in a baby's smile and in the caress of a mother's lips on a baby's forehead. You can see the sacred in the glimmer of satisfaction that comes when a student suddenly makes a breakthrough in a problem in logic. You can encounter the sacred in the tinkle of a wind chime in the wind. You can experience the sacred by raising your vision from the horizon and seeing Venus perched on the end of the new moon. It's all around us, it's just we get so caught up in the artifice of our cultural conditioning that it eludes us.

— MAX OELSCHLAEGER
In conversation with Derrick Jensen
from *Listening to the Land*

IT IS SAID BY MEN WHO KNOW ABOUT THESE THINGS that the smallest living cell probably contains over a quarter of a million protein molecules engaged in the multitudinous coördinated activities which make up the phenomenon of life. At the instant of death, whether of man or microbe, that ordered, incredible spinning passes away in an almost furious haste of those same particles to get themselves back into the chaotic, unplanned earth.

I do not think, if someone finally twists the key successfully in the tiniest and most humble house of life, that many of these questions will be answered, or that the dark forces which create lights in the deep sea and living batteries in the waters of tropical swamps, or the dread cycles of parasites, or the most noble workings of the human brain, will be much if at all revealed. Rather, I would say that if "dead" matter has reared up this curious landscape of fiddling crickets, song sparrows, and wondering men, it must be plain even to the most devoted materialist that the matter of which he speaks contains amazing, if not dreadful powers, and may not impossibly be, as Hardy has suggested, "but one mask of many worn by the Great Face behind."

— LOREN EISELEY
The Immense Journey

IN OUR RESTLESS SIGHTSEEING OF NATURE, skimming down the highway from one view to another, we see much more than we can absorb. In wilderness, we absorb much more than we see. We walk to a rhythm longer than the conscious mind can know — the rhythm of sequoias rising, the Escalante carving its canyon, the slow titanic stirring of this crust of Earth that bears us. The rhythm of the wild sounds itself in the blast of Mount St. Helens, in the boom of surf at Cape Perpetua, in shimmering aspen leaves and the hoarse whistle of a red-tailed hawk adrift in the summer sky. Life and death both dance to it: the deer browsing, the cougar snapping the deer's neck and ripping its belly, the carrion eaters transforming the cougar. The beauty of the wild is the long gesture of life in time. The beauty of skin and fur and feathers, the beauty of blood, the beauty of bones sinking into grass.

— JOHN DANIEL
"The Beauty of the Wild"
from *The Soul Unearthed*

WE ARE CONNECTED TO THE DEAD of every kind in ways not commonly remembered. The bones of the ancestors, which lie in the body of Earth, are transformed into the bodies of plants and creatures, including us. The Dineh who live in and around Chaco Canyon understand that they are an intimate part of this ancestral continuity as expressed through mountains, mists, clouds, and generating rain. They know in their bodies, in their bones, that they are directly connected to the mountains that gather the cloud, the green that gives rise to clouds, and the mist and ultimately the rain that nourishes all that grows to give forth the beautiful pollen that fertilizes and heals. In all these forms, the ancestral continuity confirms our true identity.

— JOAN HALIFAX
The Fruitful Darkness

THE SIGNIFICANCE — and ultimately the quality — of the work we do is determined by our understanding of the story in which we are taking part.

If we think of ourselves as merely biological creatures, whose story is determined by genetics or environment or history or economics or technology, then, however pleasant or painful the part we play, it cannot matter much. Its significance is that of mere self-concern. "It is a tale / Told by an idiot, full of sound and fury, / Signifying nothing," as Macbeth says when he has "supp'd full with horrors" and is "aweary of the sun."

If we think of ourselves as lofty souls trapped temporarily in lowly bodies in a dispirited, desperate, unlovable world that we must despise for Heaven's sake, then what have we done for this question of significance? If we divide reality into two parts, spiritual and material, and hold (as the Bible does *not* hold) that only the spiritual is good or desirable, then our relation to the material value that we have, in fact and for this reason, assigned to it. Thus, we become the judges and inevitably the destroyers of a world we did not make and that we are bidden to understand as a divine gift. It is impossible to see how good work might be accomplished by people who think that our life in this world either signifies nothing or has only a negative significance.

If, on the other hand, we believe that we are living souls, God's dust and God's breath, acting our parts among other creatures all made of the same dust and breath as ourselves; and if we understand that we are free, within the obvious limits of mortal human life, to do evil or good to ourselves and to the other creatures — then all our acts have a supreme significance.

— WENDELL BERRY
Sex, Freedom, and Community

EVERYONE IS THE RESULT OF FOUR FORCES: the conditions of this known-universe (matter/energy forms and ceaseless change); the biology of his species; his individual genetic heritage and the culture he's born into. Within this web of forces there are certain spaces and loops which allow to some persons the experience of inner freedom and illumination. The gradual exploration of some of these spaces is "evolution" and, for human cultures, what "history" could increasingly be. We have it within our "selves" but to change our culture. If man is to remain on earth he must transform the five-millennia-long urbanizing civilization tradition into a new ecologically sensitive harmony-oriented wild-minded scientific-spiritual culture. "Wildness is the state of complete awareness. That's why we need it."

— GARY SNYDER
Turtle Island

THE ONLY WAY TO AVERT the catastrophe of neglect is through an evolutionary leap in the way we see and feel our context. We need to experience nature and the universe *within* ourselves, not as external scenery we view outside the window of real life. In religious terms, we need to be "born again" in nature. We were baptized after our first birth into a special religious sphere that promised eternal life beyond natural boundaries. Now we need a rebirth, a connection to the nature we lost in that baptism.

It took many generations to develop a universal ethical standard for the treatment of all human beings as inherently deserving respect because all are made by the same Creator. We violate that standard routinely, but it is nonetheless an ethical organizing principle of great importance. The next step is to extend the experience of a common Creator to the natural world, and build a system of ethics, economics, and politics accordingly.

We need to see and feel ourselves in nature, not in a privileged and separate sanctuary called society. As the ecologist Aldo Leopold wrote in 1949, ethics are not simply theoretical: they involve the "loyalties, affections, and convictions" that are the very foundations of conduct. The creation of a new "land ethic" could not occur, he felt, unless the ecological issue took on a religious and philosophical character. That time has come.

— TOM HAYDEN
The Lost Gospel of the Earth

CRUELTY IS A MYSTERY, AND THE WASTE OF PAIN. But if we describe a world to compass these things, a world that is a long, brute game, then we bump against another mystery: the inrush of power and light, the canary that sings on the skull. Unless all ages and races of men have been deluded by the same mass hypnotist (who?), there seems to be such a thing as beauty, a grace wholly gratuitous. About five years ago I saw a mockingbird make a straight vertical descent from the roof gutter of a four-story building. It was an act as careless and spontaneous as the curl of a stem or the kindling of a star.

The mockingbird took a single step into the air and dropped. His wings were still folded against his sides as though he were singing from a limb and not falling, accelerating thirty-two feet per second per second, through empty air. Just a breath before he would have been dashed to the ground, he unfurled his wings with exact, deliberate care, revealing the broad bars of white, spread his elegant, white-banded tail, and so floated onto the grass. I had just rounded a corner when his insouciant step caught my eye; there was no one else in sight. The fact of his free fall was like the old philosophical conundrum about the tree that falls in the forest. The answer must be, I think, that beauty and grace are performed whether or not we will or sense them. The least we can do is try to be there.

— ANNIE DILLARD
Pilgrim at Tinker Creek

" The canary that sings on the skull "

To go into solitude, a man needs to retire as much from his chamber as from society. I am not solitary whilst I read and write, though nobody is with me. But if a man would be alone, let him look at the stars. The rays that come from those heavenly worlds will separate between him and what he touches. One might think the atmosphere was made transparent with this design, to give man, in the heavenly bodies, the perpetual presence of the sublime. Seen in the streets of cities, how great they are! If the stars should appear one night in a thousand years, how would men believe and adore; and preserve for many generations the remembrance of the city of God which had been shown! But every night come out these envoys of beauty, and light the universe with the admonishing smile.

The stars awaken a certain reverence, because though always present, they are inaccessible; but all natural objects make a kindred impression, when the mind is open to their influence. Nature never wears a mean appearance. Neither does the wisest man extort her secret, and lose his curiosity by finding out all her perfection. Nature never became a toy to a wise spirit. The flowers, the animals, the mountains, reflected the wisdom of his best hour, as much as they had delighted the simplicity of his childhood.

— RALPH WALDO EMERSON
Nature

About the Contributors

A great American iconoclast, **Edward Abbey** was born and raised on a farm in Pennsylvania and lived most of his life in the Southwest. His bestseller *The Monkey Wrench Gang* defined his confrontational and impatient response to irreverence toward the American wilderness, as did *Desert Solitaire,* his classic account of working as a ranger in what is now Arches National Park in the late 1950s. Abbey also worked as a fire lookout and part-time English professor. He died in 1989.

David Abram is an ecologist, philosopher, and accomplished sleight-of-hand magician. His remarkable book *The Spell of the Sensuous* traces the impact of the animate natural world and language on our perceptions. Abram has lived and studied with indigenous magicians in Indonesia, Nepal, and the Americas. He has received fellowships from the Watson and Rockefeller foundations and holds a Ph.D. in philosophy from the State University of New York at Stony Brook.

An imaginative chronicler of the world's splendor, **Diane Ackerman** is a poet, essayist, naturalist, and explorer. She has taught at Columbia and Cornell universities and writes for such magazines as *National Geographic,* the *New York Times,* and *The New Yorker,* where she is a staff writer. She is author of several books exploring the natural world, including *A Natural History of Love, The Moon by Whale Light, The*

Rarest of the Rare, and *A Natural History of the Senses,* which inspired the 1995 PBS series she hosted. She has also written children's books and *A Slender Thread,* a book about her experiences working a crisis line in upstate New York, where she lives. She published her sixth collection of poetry in 1998, *I Praise My Destroyer.*

A petroleum geologist who grew up in Texas, **Rick Bass** now lives in the Yaak River Valley of northwestern Montana, a region of which he has become a vociferous defender. An award-winning short fiction writer — *The Sky, the Stars, the Wilderness* and others — Bass has written two nonfiction works on wildlife, *The Ninemile Wolves,* about the reintroduction of wolves into the contiguous U.S., and *The Lost Grizzlies: A Search for Survivors in the Wilderness of Colorado.* He has also written autobiographical nonfiction: *Winter: Notes from Montana* and *Oil Notes.* His acclaimed first novel is *Where the Sea Used to Be.*

As founder and director of the Riverdale Center for Religious Research in New York, **Father Thomas Berry** is at the forefront of developing a new relationship between religion and nature. Educated as a Catholic priest, he is a cultural historian who has studied the languages and cultures of China and India. Now in his eighties, Berry is the author of *The Dream of the Earth* and coauthor, with Brian Swimme, of *The Universe Story.* The *Utne Reader* named Berry one of their 100 visionaries in 1995.

Wendell Berry left academia in 1964 and returned with his family to the place of his birth: his family's farm in Henry County, Kentucky, from which Berry became a prominent and eloquent proponent of bioregionalism and responsible small-scale farming. Berry writes fiction, poetry, and essays, including *The Unsettling of America: Culture and Agriculture,* an influential critique of commercial agriculture and the loss of local community. His most recent collection of poetry is *A Timbered Choir: The Sabbath Poems 1979–1997.*

A friend and biographer of Walt Whitman, **John Burroughs** was one of the most popular nature writers of the late 19th century. One of the first to embrace Darwin's theory of evolution, Burroughs publicly fought against anthropomorphism and emphasized scientific observation in nature writing. His more than two dozen books sold over one and a half million copies. The John Burroughs Society today owns and maintains his summer retreat, Slabsides, a National Historic Landmark in West Park, New York. The John Burroughs Medal is now given to honor excellence in nature writing.

One of the world's preeminent mythologists, **Joseph Campbell** began his career in 1934 as an instructor at Sarah Lawrence College, where he taught for almost forty years, and where the Joseph Campbell Chair in Comparative Mythology was established in his honor. He is the author of numerous books, including the bestselling *The Hero with a Thousand Faces*. His conversations with Bill Moyers from the popular television series *The Power of Myth* were collected in a bestselling book of the same name. He died in 1987.

Rachel Carson is the author of *Silent Spring*, which significantly contributed to creating an American environmental consciousness by awakening the public to the dangers of DDT in 1962. Her warning led to a federal investigation and regulation of the pesticide. Carson was a marine biologist who worked both as a specialist in fisheries and as a writer. She was also the author of *The Edge of the Sea* and *The Sea Around Us,* which won the National Book Award in 1952.

John Daniel is a poet, essayist, and environmental journalist. He has been the recipient of the Wallace Stegner Fellowship in Poetry from Stanford University, where he taught for several years and studied informally with Wallace Stegner. He has written a book of essays, *The Trail Home;* two collections of poetry, *Common Ground* and *All Things Touched by Wind;* and an exploration of his mother's descent into

Alzheimer's disease, *Looking After: A Son's Memoir*. Most recently, he has edited *Wild Song: Poems of the Natural World*, a selection of the poems he published as poetry editor of *Wilderness* magazine. He lives in the Coast Range foothills of western Oregon.

William Dietrich is a senior science reporter at the *Seattle Times*, where in 1990 he was part of a team that won a Pulitzer Prize for their coverage of the 1989 oil spill in Alaska's Prince William Sound and an examination of oil-tanker safety. He is the author of *The Final Forest: The Battle for the Last Great Trees of the Pacific Northwest* and, most recently, *Northwest Passage: The Great Columbia River*.

Annie Dillard is the author of several books, ranging from poetry *(Tickets for a Prayer Wheel)* to memoir *(An American Childhood)* to historical fiction *(The Living)* to one of the most widely lauded books of contemporary nature writing, *Pilgrim at Tinker Creek*, a chronicle of one year spent in the Blue Ridge Mountains that won the Pulitzer Prize in 1974. Dillard has taught at Wesleyan University since 1979.

Daniel Duane is the author of three books: *Lighting Out: A Vision of California and the Mountains*, a memoir about the struggles of his first year out of college and his preparations for climbing El Capitan in Yosemite; *Caught Inside: A Surfer's Year on the Pacific Coast*, about surfing while finishing his Ph.D. at the University of California, Santa Cruz; and a novel, *Looking for Mo*. Duane surfs every chance he can get and travels around the world on assignment for surfing magazines. He lives in San Francisco.

A Buddhist with experience in cowpunching and filmmaking, **Gretel Ehrlich** lives in Wyoming. She is the author of several books, including *The Solace of Open Spaces*, which won an award from the Academy of Arts and Sciences, *A Match to the Heart,* a mystical account of her recovery from a near-fatal lightning strike, and her most recent work, *Ques-*

tions of Heaven, about a Buddhist pilgrimage she took in China. Her essays appear in *Harper's*. She is currently at work on a book about Greenland.

Author of the influential bestseller *The Immense Journey,* **Loren Eiseley** was, in addition to a naturalist and writer, a professor of anthropology and Curator of Early Man at the University of Pennsylvania. His essays frequently addressed the power of the evolutionary perspective and the common ancestry shared by animals and humans. His other books include an anthology compiled during his last year, *The Star Thrower, The Unexpected Universe,* and *The Night Country*. He died in 1977.

Born in Boston in 1803, **Ralph Waldo Emerson** was an essayist and poet who left his appointment as a Unitarian minister to become one of America's most influential philosophers as the leader of the transcendental movement. After stepping down, he traveled in Europe and met with Samuel Taylor Coleridge and William Wordsworth, among others. Their influence, along with Asian religions, influenced his first book, *Nature,* which was published in 1836 and presented the essence of his mystical philosophy. He subsequently published several volumes of influential essays, including "The Over-Soul" and "Self-Reliance"; a collection of poetry; and a collection of his popular lectures. His book of essays *The Conduct of Life* was published in 1860 and became his first commercially successful work. He died in 1882.

Louise Erdrich is a novelist, poet, and Native American activist. Born in Minnesota, she is a member of the Turtle Mountain Band of Chippewa. The awards for her writing include the Nelson Algren Fiction Award, the Pushcart Prize, the American Book Award, the National Book Critics Circle Award, and the O. Henry Prize. Her books include *The Beet Queen, Love Medicine, The Bingo Palace, The Blue Jay's Dance,* and *The Crown of Columbus,* which she cowrote with her late husband, Michael Dorris. Her latest novel is *The Antelope Wife*.

Matthew Fox is the founder and president of the University of Creation Spirituality in Oakland, California. He is best-known for the recovery of the Creation Spirituality tradition, which brings together ecology, cosmology, justice, and mysticism in a theology based on "original blessing." Fox is the author of twenty-two books on culture and spirituality, including the bestselling *Original Blessing, Illuminations of Hildegard of Bingen, The Reinvention of Work,* and *Confessions,* his spiritual autobiography. He holds his Ph.D. in the history and theology of spirituality from the Institute Catholique in Paris and was formerly a Dominican priest. He has been an Episcopalian priest since 1994. In 1995, he was awarded The Peace Abbey Courage of Conscience Award.

Dan Gerber is a writer from northern Michigan whose works include three novels, *American Atlas, Out of Control,* and *A Voice from the River;* a collection of short stories, *Grass Fires;* and five books of poetry. His poems, stories, and essays have appeared in many publications, including *The New Yorker, The Partisan Review, Sports Illustrated, New Letters,* and *The Georgia Review.*

A writer and English professor, **Paul Gruchow** lives on a farm in Northfield, Minnesota. He is the author of *Boundary Waters: The Grace of the Wild* and *Grass Roots: The Universe of Home,* as well as many articles in publications such as *Nature Conservancy, Hungry Mind Review,* and the *Utne Reader.* He is a frequent speaker on rural land issues and literature.

John Haines is a poet, essayist, and naturalist who homesteaded along the Tanana River in central Alaska for twenty-two years. He is the author of many collections of poetry, and two autobiographical works, including *The Stars, the Snow, the Fire: Twenty-Five Years in the Alaska Wilderness.* Formerly Alaska's poet laureate, he has taught at several universities and has received numerous awards, including two Guggenheim Fellowships, a National Endowment for the Arts Fellowship, and the Fellowship of the Academy of American Poets.

Joan Halifax is a visionary thinker who synthesizes Buddhism, shamanism, anthropology, mythology, and deep ecology. A student and colleague of Joseph Campbell and Thich Nhat Hanh, she is author of *Shaman: The Wounded Healer*, and coauthor, with Stanislav Grof, of *The Human Encounter with Death*. She was the founder of an educational community called The Ojai Foundation.

A poet, novelist, essayist, and screenwriter, **Jim Harrison**'s wide-ranging interests run from Zen Buddhism and gourmet cooking to social commentary and wilderness preservation. He is the author of *The Woman Lit by Fireflies, Julip,* and *Legends of the Fall,* all collections of three novellas each. His novels include *Sundog, Warlock,* and *Dalva;* his books of poetry include *After Ikkyu and other Poems* and *The Theory and Practice of Rivers and New Poems. Just Before Dark* collects his essays on literature, food, travel, and sport. His most recent novel is *The Road Home.* He lives with his family on a farm in northern Michigan.

A nature writer and conservationist centered in Cape Cod, Massachusetts, since 1942, **John Hay** has written several seminal works of natural history and nature essays. His books include *The Run,* which follows the migration cycle of herrings, *The Great Beach,* for which he won the John Burroughs Medal, *In Defense of Nature, The Undiscovered Country,* and *The Immortal Wilderness.* Hay taught Nature Writing and Nature and Human Values at Dartmouth College for fifteen years. His most recent book of essays is *In the Company of Light.*

Long an environmental and political activist, **Tom Hayden** is a member of the California State Senate, where he is the chairman of its Natural Resources and Wildlife Committee. He was a founder of Students for a Democratic Society and a member of the Chicago Seven. He has lectured widely on ecotheology, a primary subject of his book *The Lost Gospel of the Earth: A Call for Renewing Nature, Spirit, and Politics.* He lives in Santa Monica, California.

James Hillman is an author and depth psychologist who has taught at Yale, Syracuse, the University of Chicago, and the University of Dallas, where he cofounded the Dallas Institute for the Humanities and Culture. He has written more than twenty books, including *Re-Visioning Psychology, A Blue Fire,* and *Kinds of Power: A Guide to Its Intelligent Uses.* His latest bestseller is *The Soul's Code: In Search of Character and Calling.*

Until recently, **Edward Hoagland** divided his time between New York City, where he was born, and a farmhouse without electricity in Barton, Vermont. These dual sensibilities of nature and city are reflected in the wide-ranging subjects of his essays. His first novel, *Cat Man,* won Hoagland a Houghton Mifflin Literary Fellowship as he was graduating from Harvard in 1956. He has written three novels since, the most recent being *Seven Rivers West* in 1986. His essays appear in *Harper's, The Atlantic,* the *Village Voice,* and many other periodicals.

A Chickasaw writer of award-winning fiction and poetry, **Linda Hogan** teaches at the University of Colorado at Boulder. Her novel *Mean Spirit* received the Oklahoma Book Award for fiction, the Mountains and Plains Booksellers Award, and was a finalist for the Pulitzer Prize in 1991. She has published several books of poetry, including *Seeing through the Sun,* which received an American Book Award, and *The Book of Medicines,* a finalist for the National Book Award. Her book of nonfiction is *Dwellings: A Spiritual History of the Living World.* She is coeditor, with Deena Metzger and Brenda Peterson, of *Intimate Nature: The Bond Between Women and Animals.* Her latest novel is *Power.*

Formerly a librarian at Brown University, **Sue Hubbell** later became a beekeeper and writer in the Ozarks of Missouri. Her first book, *A Country Year,* tells the story of her awakening to the nature surrounding her rural home as she coped with a recent divorce. Hubbell's book *Far-flung*

Hubbell is a collection of her travel essays from *The New Yorker*. She has also written two books on bugs, *A Book of Bees* and *Broadsides from the Other Orders: A Book of Bugs*, both of which were recently reissued.

Sam Keen is an author, teacher, and the former editor of *Psychology Today*, who has been conducting seminars on personal mythology for twenty years. He attended Harvard Divinity School and received his Ph.D. from Princeton in 1962. Keen has taught at the Louisville Presbyterian Seminary, Prescott College, and the Humanistic Philosophy Institute. He is the author of *Fire in the Belly, Hymns to an Unknown God*, and, most recently, *To Love and Be Loved*. He lives on a ranch in Sonoma, California.

A professional forester, **Aldo Leopold** described a year on his Wisconsin farm in the posthumously published *A Sand County Almanac*, which became one of the key works in developing environmental awareness. Leopold's "Land Ethic" extended the idea of an interdependent community to include "soils, waters, plants, and animals." One of the founders of the Wilderness Society, Leopold taught at the University of Wisconsin, where he invented the field of game management. He was an advisor to the United Nations on conservation when he died fighting a brush fire on a neighbor's farm in 1948.

Barry Lopez, one of the preeminent nature writers of this century, lives and writes in the Cascade Mountains of Oregon. He is the author of *Arctic Dreams*, winner of the National Book Award, *Of Wolves and Men*, an extraordinary exploration of man's ambivalent relationship with wildlife, and several collections of short fiction, including *Field Notes* and *Winter Count*. Lopez is a contributing editor to *Harper's*. He has won the Award in Literature from the American Academy of Arts and Letters and the John Burroughs Medal, among other honors. His latest book of nonfiction is *About This Life: Journeys on the Edge of Memory*.

Peter Matthiessen, after cofounding the *Paris Review* upon graduating from Yale, went on to become one of the foremost novelists and nature writers of his generation. In addition to writing such novels as *Far Tortuga* and *At Play in the Fields of the Lord,* which was made into a motion picture, he has written over a dozen books on wildlife and the natural world, including *The Snow Leopard,* an account of his journey in the Nepali Himalaya, which won the National Book Award. His latest novel is *Lost Man's River*. He writes and teaches Zen Buddhism from his home on Long Island.

A long-time staff writer at *The New Yorker,* **Bill McKibben** is the author of the landmark work about the philosophical and environmental impact of humankind's influence on the earth's climate, *The End of Nature*. His follow-up, *Hope, Human and Wild,* examined three places where people are working to improve their environment. His writing on nature has appeared in *The New York Review of Books,* the *New York Times, Rolling Stone,* and other national publications. His latest book is *Maybe One: A Personal and Environmental Argument for Single-Child Families*. He lives with his wife and daughter in the Adirondack Mountains of New York.

Thomas Merton lived for almost thirty years as a Trappist monk at the Abbey of Our Lady of Gethsemani near Bardstown, Kentucky. His prolific and wide-ranging writing included essays, poetry, novels, and his autobiography, *The Seven Storey Mountain*. Among the themes in his work were explorations of monastic life and Eastern religious traditions. He died in 1968, while traveling in Thailand.

Kathleen Dean Moore is chair of the department of philosophy at Oregon State University in Corvallis, Oregon. She holds a doctorate in the philosophy of law from the University of Colorado and is the author of two textbooks that connect critical thinking and effective writing. Her book *Riverwalking: Reflections on Moving Water* is a collection of essays about philosophy and nature.

John Muir was born in 1838 in Dunbar, Scotland. In 1949 he emigrated with his family to the United States, and later studied natural sciences at the University of Wisconsin. He explored forests and wild lands throughout the world, from Alaska and South America, to Russia, Siberia, and the Philippines. He eventually settled in California and became a crusader to save the forested land of the high Sierra, including the landscape in and around the Yosemite Valley, which led to his founding of the Sierra Club in 1892. His writings on these areas formed two of his classic books, *The Mountains of California* and *My First Summer in the Sierra*. Muir Woods National Monument in Marin County, California, was established in 1908. Muir died in 1914.

Gary Paul Nabhan is a cofounder of Native Seeds/SEARCH, which works to conserve native crops and plants. He holds a doctorate in ethnobotany from the University of Arizona, Tucson. His books include *The Forgotten Pollinators; Songbirds, Truffles, and Wolves; The Desert Smells Like Rain; Enduring Seeds;* and *Gathering the Desert,* for which he won a John Burroughs Medal for Nature Writing. He has also been awarded a MacArthur Fellowship and a Pew Scholarship for conservation research. He lives in Arizona.

Richard Nelson combines the interests and attentions of nature writer and cultural anthropologist in his writings about Alaska and its native people. His books of ethnography, *Hunters of the Northern Ice* and *Make Prayers to the Raven,* study the Koyukon people of Alaska and their relationship with hunting and the land. His more personal book of natural memoir, *The Island Within,* won the John Burroughs Award in 1991. His most recent book, *Heart and Blood: Living with Deer in America,* examines our complex relationship with one of the continent's most pervasive animals.

Kent Nerburn holds a Ph.D. in religion and art from the Graduate Theological Seminary in Berkeley, California, and is a sculptor with works in such diverse settings as the Peace Museum in Hiroshima, Japan, and Westminster Benedictine Abbey in Mission, British Columbia. For several years he worked with the Ojibwe of northern Minnesota, helping collect the memories of the tribal elders. He is the author of *A Haunting Reverence, Letters to My Son* and the award-winning *Neither Wolf nor Dog*. He lives with his wife and family in northern Minnesota.

Frequently associated with the American Southwest and his earth-centered, radical politics, **John Nichols** is a writer and photographer who lives in Taos, New Mexico. His writing career began in 1965 when, at the age of 22, his first novel *The Sterile Cuckoo* was published and made into a film starring Liza Minnelli. His acclaimed New Mexico Trilogy began in 1974 with the publication of *The Milagro Beanfield War*, which was adapted into a film by Robert Redford. Nichols combines his nonfiction writing and photography in *The Sky's the Limit* and *Keep It Simple*.

Max Oelschlaeger is professor of philosophy and religious studies at the University of North Texas. He is the author of *Caring for Creation: An Ecumenical Approach to the Environmental Crisis, The Environmental Imperative: A Socio-Economic Perspective*, and the influential landmark work on Western culture's attitudes toward wilderness, *The Idea of Wilderness*.

Ohiyesa was born in 1858 in the Santee Sioux or Dakota tribe of southern Minnesota. When he was four, the tribe's uprising against the U.S. government was squelched and Ohiyesa's father, Many Lightnings, was captured. Ohiyesa was taken in by his uncle and raised in the traditional Dakota ways until his father returned from a government internment camp. Having experienced the power of the encroaching white world, Many Lightnings encouraged his son to enter it. Ohiyesa began studies at Beloit College in Wisconsin and became Charles Alexander Eastman. He went on to receive a B.A. from Dartmouth in 1887 and an M.D. from Boston University in 1890. He established thirty-two Young Men's Christian Association Indian groups and helped found the Boy Scouts and Campfire Girls. He became an outspoken educator and activist for American Indian rights and wrote several books, including *The Soul of the Indian.* He died in 1939.

Mary Oliver is a poet and professor who has won the Pulitzer Prize and the National Book Award, among other awards, for her poetry. In addition to her poetry, she is the author of *A Poetry Handbook,* an introduction to writing poetry, *Rules for the Dance: A Handbook for Writing and Reading Metrical Verse,* as well as *Blue Pastures,* a book of prose essays. Her most recent collection of poetry and prose poetry is *West Wind.* She teaches at Bennington College in Vermont.

Brenda Peterson has had a varied career as novelist, editorial assistant for *The New Yorker,* fiction editor for *Rocky Mountain Magazine,* and environmental writer. Her first novel, *River of Light,* was published by Knopf in 1978. Since then she has written two more novels, *Becoming the Enemy* and *Duck and Cover.* She has written two books of nature essays, *Living by Water* and *Nature and Other Mothers,* and one nonfiction work, *Sister Stories.* She is coeditor, with Linda Hogan and Deena Metzger, of *Intimate Nature: The Bond Between Women and Animals.* She lives on Puget Sound in Seattle.

Michael Pollan is the author of *Second Nature: A Gardener's Education* and *A Place of My Own: The Education of an Amateur Builder,* which describes the adventure of building of a small writing hut behind his house. He is editor at large of *Harper's,* where he has written such articles as "Why Mow?" and "Opium, Made Easy: One Gardener's Encounter with the War on Drugs" about the questionable legality of garden-variety poppies. He is a contributing writer to *The New York Times*

Magazine, and a columnist for *Home & Garden,* where he writes about architecture. Pollan lives in Cornwall Bridge, Connecticut, with his wife, the painter Judith Belzer, and their son Isaac.

David Quammen's book *The Song of the Dodo: Island Biogeography in the Age of Extinction* is an epic travelogue that explores how dividing the natural world into small, isolated patches of landscape is bringing many of the world's species to the brink of extinction. Since 1981, Quammen's eclectic and entertaining column on biology and nature, "Natural Acts," has appeared in *Outside* magazine. These essays are collected in *The Flight of the Iguana* and *Wild Thoughts from Wild Places.* He lives with his wife, a biologist, in Bozeman, Montana.

C.L. Rawlins was born and lives in Wyoming, west of the Wind River Range. His books include *In Gravity National Park: Poems* (1998), *Broken Country: Mountains & Memory* (1996), and *Sky's Witness: A Year in the Wind River Range* (1993). In addition to various literary prizes, he received the U.S. Forest Service Primitive Skills Award for a field study of acid deposition in the Bridger Wilderness. He now serves as president of the Wyoming Outdoor Council.

Chet Raymo is professor of physics and astronomy at Stonehill College in Massachusetts. A teacher, naturalist, and science columnist for the *Boston Globe,* he is the author of the highly praised *The Soul of the Night,* the bestselling *365 Starry Nights* and several other books, including a novel, *The Dork of Cork.* Based in the landscape of the Dingle Peninsula in western Ireland, Raymo's book *Honey from Stone: A Naturalist's Search for God* fell out of print and was recently reissued by the Hungry Mind Press in Minneapolis. His latest book is *Skeptics and True Believers: The Exhilarating Connection Between Science and Religion.*

Sy Safransky is the founder and editor of *The Sun,* a monthly magazine of essays, fiction, interviews, poetry, and photographs now in its twenty-fifth year of publication. His essays from *The Sun* are collected in *Four in the Morning*. Safransky is also the editor of three collections of writings from the magazine: *Sun Beams: A Book of Quotations* and *A Bell Ringing in the Empty Sky: The Best of the Sun Volumes 1 & 2*. He lives in Chapel Hill, North Carolina.

An award-winning essayist, **Scott Russell Sanders** is professor of English at Indiana University. He is the author of fifteen books, including eight works of fiction and several collections of essays. His writing has appeared in *Omni, Harper's, Orion,* the *New York Times, North American Review, Georgia Review, Parabola,* and the *Utne Reader*. He has served as literary editor of *The Cambridge Review* at Cambridge University, where he received his Ph.D. in English in 1971.

Paul Shepard was a professor of human ecology at Pitzer College in Claremont, California. Among his many books, his influential *Nature and Madness* posited an early connection between human psychology and environmental destruction. Along with *The Tender Carnivore and the Sacred Game* and *Thinking Animals, Nature & Madness* was recently rereleased by the University of Georgia Press. Shepard also taught at Smith and Dartmouth. He died in 1996.

Gary Snyder, an original member of the beat generation, is a poet and essayist. Since 1985 he has taught literature and wilderness thought at the University of California at Davis. He is the author of sixteen books, including *Turtle Island,* which won the Pulitzer Prize for poetry in 1975, *No Nature,* a finalist for the National Book Award, *The Practice of the Wild, A Place in Space,* and the epic poem *Mountains and Rivers Without End*. He lives with his wife and family in the Sierra Nevada foothills in northern California.

Mentor to such writers as Wendell Berry and John Daniel, **Wallace Stegner** was a professor of English and director of the Creative Writing

Program at Stanford, as well as a renowned novelist, essayist, and short story writer. Among the many awards he received for his writing, he won the Pulitzer Prize in 1972 for *Angle of Repose,* and the National Book Award in 1977 for *The Spectator Bird.* After teaching at Utah, Wisconsin, Iowa, and Harvard, Stegner returned to the West of his upbringing — the predominant theme of both his fiction and conservation writing. He died in 1993 at age 84 after an auto accident.

Mathematical cosmologist **Brian Swimme** received his Ph.D. from the University of Oregon in 1978. He is the author of *The Hidden Heart of the Cosmos: Humanity and the New Story, The Universe Is a Green Dragon: A Cosmic Creation Story,* and *The Universe Story,* which resulted from a ten-year collaboration with Father Thomas Berry. His work was featured in the three-part BBC television series, *Soul of the Universe,* along with such physicists as Stephen Hawking and Ilya Prigogine. He teaches at the Institute of Integral Studies in San Francisco.

Bron Taylor is Oshkosh Foundation Professor of Religion and Social Ethics at the University of Wisconsin Oshkosh, where he is the founding director of its environmental studies program. He publishes widely on environmental movements and environmental ethics. His books include *Ecological Resistance Movements: The Global Emergence of Radical and Popular Environmentalism* (SUNY Press, 1995) and the forthcoming *On Sacred Ground: Earth First! and Environmental Ethics* (Beacon Press).

A distinguished medical doctor, **Lewis Thomas** was the president of the Memorial Sloane-Kettering Cancer Center from 1973 to 1980. His essays first appeared in *The New England Journal of Medicine.* His first book of essays, *The Lives of a Cell: Notes of a Biology Watcher,* was published in 1974 and won the National Book Award. He is the author of three more books of essays, *Late Night Thoughts on Listening to Mahler's Ninth Symphony, The Medusa and the Snail,* and *The Youngest Science.*

With his claim that "in Wildness is the preservation of the world," American writer, philosopher, and naturalist **Henry David Thoreau** may be the father of modern conservationism. Born in Concord, Massachusetts, in 1817, Thoreau lived to see only two of his written works published: *A Week on the Concord and Merrimack Rivers,* which described a boat trip with his older brother, and his masterpiece, *Walden,* a profound philosophical exploration of more than two solitary years at Walden Pond, outside Concord. Thoreau spent a night in jail after he refused to pay his poll tax in protest of the Mexican War. He expressed this political philosophy in his influential essay "Civil Disobedience." Thoreau died in 1862, after a battle with tuberculosis.

Stephen Trimble has worked as a park ranger in Arches National Park, a photographer, and a writer. He is the author of *The Sagebrush Ocean: A Natural History of the Great Basin,* which won the Sierra Club's Ansel Adams Award and The High Desert Museum's Chiles Award, among many other books; coauthor, with Gary Paul Nabhan, of *The Geography of Childhood: Why Children Need Wild Places;* and editor of *Words from the Land: Encounters with Natural History Writing.* His nature photography has been featured in dozens of books and magazines. He lives in Salt Lake City.

Now the chief climbing guide for a mountaineering school in Grand Teton National Park, **Jack Turner** is the author of *The Abstract Wild* and an upcoming book on the Tetons. Turner taught philosophy at the University of Illinois at Chicago until he decided to leave academia for a more adventurous life. He has been climbing for thirty-six years in the American West and has led or participated in expeditions in Pakistan, India, Nepal, Tibet, China, and Peru. He lives on a ranch near the Mexican border and in Grand Teton National Park.

David Rains Wallace is the author of *The Klamath Knot, The Quetzal and the Macaw,* and *Adventuring in Central America.* He is a recipient of the John Burroughs Medal for Nature Writing and a former fellow with the National Endowment for the Arts and the Fulbright Foundation. His latest book is *The Monkey's Bridge: Mysteries of Evolution in Central America.* His articles have appeared in *Wilderness, Sierra, Harper's,* and the *New York Times,* among other publications. He lives in Berkeley, California.

The great American romantic poet **Walt Whitman** was born on Long Island in 1819 and raised in Brooklyn. After leaving school at twelve, he began working for New York newspapers, eventually editing and writing for several, and starting *The Long Islander* in 1938. Very influenced by Emerson's transcendentalism, as well as his wide-ranging reading, Whitman was an enthusiastic, tolerant, political writer who was fired from the *Brooklyn Eagle* for speaking out against slavery in 1848. After failing to find a publisher for his first twelve poems, in 1855 Whitman self-published *Leaves of Grass,* which became recognized as one of the great works of American literature in the decades after his death. He continued to revise and republish *Leaves of Grass* throughout his life, along with other poetry and prose. Whitman died in 1892.

Terry Tempest Williams grew up in a Mormon family in Utah. Her experience in that culture and its relationship with the land form the foundation of her bestselling book *Refuge: An Unnatural History of Family and Place,* which, among many themes, tells the story of her mother's battle with cancer and its possible cause in nuclear weapon testing. Her essays appear in *Harper's, Outside, Orion,* and other publications, and are collected in *An Unspoken Hunger: Stories from the Field.*

Edward O. Wilson is Pellegrino University Professor and curator in entomology at the Museum of Comparative Zoology at Harvard University. An entomologist known for his study of ants, he is the author of two Pulitzer Prize–winning books, *On Human Nature* and *The Ants* (with Bert Hölldobler), and many other works, including *Biophilia,*

Sociobiology, and *The Diversity of Life.* He is a tireless educator on the importance of biodiversity and one of the creators of sociobiology, a controversial field of science that explores the biological basis of social behavior. His latest bestseller is *Consilience: The Unity of Knowledge,* in which he undertakes the task of building common ground between academic disciplines through science.

Contributor Index

Permissions Acknowledgments

Grateful acknowledgment is given to the following publishers and copyright holders for permission to reprint the quotations in The Sacred Earth:

EDWARD ABBEY: Excerpts from *Desert Solitaire* by Edward Abbey. Copyright © 1968 by Edward Abbey, renewed 1996 by Clarke Abbey. Reprinted by permission of Don Congdon Associates, Inc. Excerpt from *Appalachian Wilderness* by Edward Abbey, photographs by Eliot Porter. Copyright © 1970 by E.P. Dutton, Inc. Reprinted by permission of Dutton Signet, a division of Penguin Books USA Inc.

DAVID ABRAM: Excerpts from *The Spell of the Sensuous* by David Abram. Copyright © 1996 by David Abram. Reprinted by permission of Pantheon Books, a division of Random House, Inc.

DIANE ACKERMAN: Excerpt from *A Natural History of the Senses* by Diane Ackerman. Copyright © 1990 by Diane Ackerman. Reprinted by permission of Random House, Inc. Excerpt from *The Rarest of the Rare* by Diane Ackerman. Copyright © 1995 by Diane Ackerman. Reprinted by permission of Random House, Inc.

RICK BASS: Excerpt from *The Ninemile Wolves* by Rick Bass. Copyright © 1993 by Rick Bass. Reprinted by permission of Clark City Press, Inc. Excerpts from *Winter: Notes from Montana* by Rick Bass. Copyright © 1991 by Rick Bass. Reprinted by permission of Houghton Mifflin Company/Seymour Lawrence. All rights reserved. Excerpt from *The Book of Yaak*. Copyright © 1996 by Rick Bass. Reprinted by permission of Houghton Mifflin Company. All rights reserved.

THOMAS BERRY: Excerpts from *The Dream of the Earth* by Thomas Berry. Copyright © 1988 by Thomas Berry. Reprinted by permission of Sierra Club Books. Excerpts

Inc., Bill McKibben, and the Watkins/Loomis Agency. Excerpt from *The Age of Missing Information* by William McKibben. Copyright © 1992 by William McKibben. Reprinted by permission of Random House, Inc.

THOMAS MERTON: Excerpt from *Raids on the Unspeakable* by Thomas Merton. Copyright © 1966 by The Abbey of Gethsemani, Inc. Reprinted by permission of New Directions Publishing Corp. and Laurence Pollinger Limited.

KATHLEEN DEAN MOORE: Excerpt from *Riverwalking* by Kathleen Dean Moore. Copyright © 1995 by Kathleen Dean Moore. Reprinted by permission of The Lyons Press.

GARY PAUL NABHAN: Excerpt from *Cultures of Habitat: On Nature, Culture, and Story* by Gary Paul Nabhan. Copyright © 1997 by Gary Paul Nabhan. Reprinted by permission of Counterpoint.

RICHARD NELSON: Excerpts from *The Island Within* by Richard Nelson. Copyright © 1989 by Richard Nelson. Published by Vintage Books, a division of Random House, Inc., New York and originally by North Point Press. Reprinted by permission of Susan Bergholz Literary Services, New York. All rights reserved. Excerpt from "Life-Ways of the Hunter" from *Talking on the Water: Conversations About Nature and Creativity* by Jonathan White. Copyright © 1994 by Jonathan White. Reprinted by permission of Sierra Club Books.

KENT NERBURN: Excerpts from *A Haunting Reverence: Meditations on a Northern Land* by Kent Nerburn. Copyright © 1996 by Kent Nerburn. Reprinted by permission of New World Library.

JOHN NICHOLS: Excerpts from *The Sky's the Limit: A Defense of the Earth* by John Nichols. Copyright © 1990 by John Nichols. Reprinted by permission of W.W. Norton & Company, Inc.

MAX OELSCHLAEGER: Excerpt from *Listening to the Land: Conversations About Nature, Culture, and Eros* by Derrick Jensen. Copyright © 1995 by Derrick Jensen. Reprinted by permission of Sierra Club Books.

MARY OLIVER: Excerpts from *Blue Pastures* by Mary Oliver. Copyright © 1995 by Mary Oliver. Reprinted by permission of Harcourt Brace, Inc.

BRENDA PETERSON: Excerpts from *Living by Water: True Stories of Nature and Spirit* by Brenda Peterson. Copyright © 1990, 1994 by Brenda Peterson. Reprinted by permission of the author and Ballantine Books.

MICHAEL POLLAN: Excerpt from *A Place of My Own* by Michael Pollan. Copyright © 1997 by Michael Pollan. Reprinted by permission of Random House, Inc.

169

About the Editor

Jason Gardner is managing editor at New World Library. He has worked as an environmental journalist, English teacher, bookseller, and book editor, and has traveled extensively in Latin America and Asia. He received a bachelor's degree in English from Grinnell College in Iowa and a master's degree in journalism from the University of Illinois at Urbana-Champaign. He lives in Berkeley, California.

About David Brower

Born in Berkeley, California, in 1912, **David Brower** is the founder and chairman of Earth Island Institute and has been fighting conservation battles since 1938. Mr. Brower joined the Sierra Club in 1933, became a member of its board of directors in 1941, and was its first executive director from 1952 to 1969. He saw the club's membership grow from 2,000 to 77,000 before leaving on request in 1969, when he founded Friends of the Earth and the League of Conservation Voters. As a climber and mountaineer, Brower made seventy first ascents in Yosemite, the High Sierra, and on Shiprock in New Mexico. He has been nominated for the Nobel Peace Prize three times, and awarded the Blue Planet Award in Japan.

About The Wilderness Society

In 1935, a small but dedicated group of conservationists — including Aldo Leopold and Robert Marshall — formed a new organization to protect and preserve America's wild places before they vanished. They called the organization the Wilderness Society. And they put out an urgent call for "spirited people who will fight for the freedom of the wilderness."

Nearly 30 years later, President Lyndon B. Johnson signed the Wilderness Act into law. Today, Americans enjoy some 104 million acres of protected wilderness, due in large part to the efforts of the Wilderness Society.

The Wilderness Society is a nonprofit, 250,000-member organization dedicated to creating a nationwide network of wild lands and fostering an American land ethic.

Four percent of the publisher's proceeds from *The Sacred Earth* will be donated to the Wilderness Society. To join us in supporting them, please contact:

THE WILDERNESS SOCIETY
900 Seventeenth St. N.W.
Washington D.C., 20006-2598
(202) 833-2300 OR
1-800-THE-WILD
member@wilderness.org
http://www.wilderness.org

NEW WORLD LIBRARY is dedicated to publishing books and cassettes that inspire and challenge us to improve the quality of our lives and our world. Our books and cassettes are available at bookstores everywhere. For a complete catalog, contact:

NEW WORLD LIBRARY
14 Pamaron Way
Novato, California 94949

Phone: (415) 884-2100
Fax: (415) 884-2199

Or call toll free: (800) 972-6657
Catalog requests: Ext. 50
Ordering: Ext. 52

E-mail: escort@nwlib.com
http://www.nwlib.com